Heart & Home

CATHERINE CARTON is the lady behind the award-winning interiors and lifestyle blog daintydressdiaries.com. She is a lover of upcycling, recycling and making the old new again.

Dainty Dress Diaries was created in 2014. While brain-dumping potential names with a workmate, Catherine and her pal decided to go with 'Dainty' because Catherine is 4'11", 'Dress' because all she wore was cute dresses, and 'Diaries' so that the blog could cover a wide range of topics. In the beginning, Catherine mostly blogged about vintage style, fashion and homeware, but over the years she has become known for her warm personality and the unique creative projects she shares with her online community.

Her first book for The O'Brien Press was the bestselling *Dainty Dress Diaries* (2022).
www.daintydressdiaries.com
www.youtube.com/daintydiaries
www.instagram.com/daintydressdiaries

Heart & Home

*Craft and DIY projects to bring love
into your house and garden*

Text and
photographs
by

Catherine Carton

THE O'BRIEN PRESS
DUBLIN

First published 2024 by The O'Brien Press Ltd.,
12 Terenure Road East, Rathgar, Dublin 6, D06 HD27, Ireland.
Tel: +353 1 4923333. Fax: +353 1 4922777
Email: books@obrien.ie. Website: obrien.ie
The O'Brien Press is a member of Publishing Ireland.

ISBN 978-1-78849-421-2

10 9 8 7 6 5 4 3 2 1
28 27 26 25 24

Printed and bound by Drukarnia Skleniarz, Poland.
The paper in this book is produced using pulp from managed forests.

This is a DIY book, and all projects involve a degree of risk. Every effort has been
made to ensure that all the information in this book is accurate. However, since
conditions, tools, materials and skills will vary, the publisher and author cannot
be responsible for any injury, loss or damage that may result from the use of the
information in this book.

Published in

For Jack & Lily,

for showing me the magic of the world through your eyes

While I have so many people to thank, I want to begin by thanking you. The person who has bought this book, or maybe you are standing in a bookshop and having a flick through. I hope these pages become a source of inspiration, information, and, above all, a companion on your journey of putting heart into your home.

A village put this book together, and I want to thank all the team at The O'Brien Press for their support. To Ivan and Kunak for having faith in me. A special thank you to my editor, Nicola. We had many cups of tea and brainstorming sessions in my back garden as we pieced this project together. A big thank you to Emma for her stunning design work, which breathes life into every page. To Susan for her advice on the sewing projects. To Elena, Brenda, Ruth, Chloe and Gabbie: thank you for getting this book into as many hands as possible, and for making the whole process fun!

I give heartfelt thanks to all my family members for their unwavering support over the years. I am grateful to the beautiful circle of women who consistently uplift, lend a listening ear, and create a nurturing space for my growth. Your presence during triumphs and challenges means the world to me. A special shoutout to Karen, Joanne, Rachel, Adele, Greta & Chloe.

And finally, thank you to the online community that stands by me every day. Whether it's with a kind comment, valuable feedback or inspiring ideas, you fill my heart with gratitude. Your willingness to share my message and accompany me on this creative journey means more to me than words can express. Thank you for being an integral part of this beautiful adventure.

Níl aon tinteán mar do thinteán féin

Contents

Introduction

When I was asked to think of a title for this book, I struggled. I wanted to get across the idea of putting heart and love into your home, but I know that for many, especially nowadays, 'home' can be a stressful concept. No amount of piped cushions or DIY diffusers can ease the pain of high rents, interest rates and a dire housing market.

But I've always found comfort in tweaking whatever space I'm in, whether it was rearranging my bedroom as a kid, a fresh lick of paint after a breakup, or new bedsheets … just because.

And so I began to think about the idea of home. What makes a home? Is it a particular smell, or a feeling? Have you ever walked into a show house or a fancy office block and it felt empty? Like it was missing something.

Houses become homes when we fill them with treasures we find along the way, and when we make memories inside those four walls. I love it when old houses have wallpaper stripped and you get to see the layers of paper underneath, how each layer holds memories, and how the wall could tell a story if it could speak.

My own home journey led me here to this book. Like many others, after buying my house, I didn't have a reno budget. In fact, I barely had enough for a kettle and toaster set! Over the last decade, I flexed my creative muscles, tried many different crafts and learned new skills (and failed at some) to create a home that gives me a feeling of calm and joy when I return to it each day. Over time, I put heart into my house, which became my home.

Throughout this book, I want to inspire you to get creative and love your space, whatever size it may be, wherever you are on your journey. Start right now by asking yourself, what do you think puts heart into your home?

A little letter on my learns

In the time between my first book and this one, I took part in two new classes in my local area: woodworking and an art class. I was anxious to start something new but also crazy excited, and before attending, my head was bursting with all these big project ideas.

I was humbled on my first day in both classes to find out how much I had to learn, and so I began with the basics. I spent three hours cutting wood with a hand saw in my first woodwork class, and in my first art class, I spent hours drawing shapes.

Sometimes when we try to create something new, we see the end point in our minds, and if we don't achieve it quickly and perfectly, it can knock our confidence. The joy really is in the journey when it comes to working on your home and tackling a new project.

If it's your first time to drill a hole, sew, stain or paint, take some time to drill holes on a scrap piece of wood, grab old pieces of fabric and sew straight lines, get comfy with a paintbrush and take a little extra time to practise before tackling bigger jobs.

For example, if you want to create wall panelling, like on page 119, why not try making wooden frames for pictures, like on page 44, first? By doing this smaller project, you get a feel for the material, and if you are like me, you'll realise it's harder to cut than it looks in YouTube videos! Practise measuring and cutting your mitre corners with that smaller project before stepping up to an entire room of wall panelling.

Mistakes are welcome around here

As they say, mistakes are your best teachers, and I know from experience that accidentally sewing the wrong sides of fabric together or sticking your stool leg on wonky will teach you more than this book or any online tutorial will. You learn your best lessons when you have the patience to problem-solve and see where you went wrong.

My weekly woodworking classes also taught me about 'progress over perfection'. Yes, it's cheesy enough to put on a motivational mug, but it is very true! Each week, as my cuts got straighter and my hand was less shaky with the chisel, it was a win. Two months in, I was proud as punch with my stool, but I was prouder for giving myself that time to show up each week to practise.

When trying something new, be extra kind to yourself. That inner critic can rear its head and fill us with doubting thoughts. As my favourite painter Bob Ross used to say, anything you're willing to practise, you can do.

I still battle with my inner perfectionist, although these days it's more of a friendly squabble. She rears her head when I try something for the first time, when I want to be good at it immediately, with no mistakes. I want to run before I can walk, sew a cushion before I can thread a needle, and I want my seeds to sprout tomorrow.

If you are anything like me, try to remember that it's not all about the end result. In other words, take pride in your progress. If you're doing a straightforward project like the headband on page 99, why not sew a few of them (they make lovely gifts), compare them, and see how your stitches improve after each one?

I do this each year in the garden. When something grows differently than expected, I will plant it in another spot the following season, enjoying the journey and not seeking perfection.

Finding time in a hectic world

I have heard myself say, 'But I don't have the time to learn that' or 'I don't have time to practise'. Absolutely, yes, there are busy periods in our lives when we can't (or shouldn't) take on any more. Even energetically, we all have our winter seasons where we might not have the energy to try something new, and that's okay. But there are also times when we think we are too busy, when in fact, we are overstimulated by our phones, work email and streaming TV. (Guilty as charged.)

We make time to go to the gym or outdoors to exercise our physical bodies, but watch what magic can happen if you exercise your creativity for two or three hours a week, at a class or just noodling around for practice.

Throughout this book, I have smaller projects that you can do in a shorter time, perfect for when you have an hour or two for yourself to create.

Creating on a budget

Taking up a new skill can be costly, but I know from experience that there are dusty toolboxes on shed shelves, sewing machines in friends' attics, and second-hand sites bursting with nearly new craft supplies that people are passing on. Reach out to others and ask to borrow things, as most people are very happy to help out. Myself and my neighbour are regular plant swappers and often give each other soil, divided plants and wheelbarrow lends.

Sometimes, renting a tool can be more cost-effective, especially if you don't have loads of storage space. For example, rent a saw the first time you're doing a big DIY project; if you find yourself hooked, you can then invest in one.

Always look around your house before heading to the shops. Old curtains and bedsheets are perfect for many sewing projects, and pallet wood can be great to practise on. I still buy new things, and when I do, it feels like such a treat, but I get more of a buzz when I can reuse something old.

Also, don't be afraid to ask for help. Wallpapering is more fun when there are two people, and problem-solving a mitred corner can be easier with a friend. I would love it if you shared a project in this book with a good friend and tried it together.

And lastly, take all these ideas and make them your own. I say this often on my YouTube channel, but I really do mean it. Tweak measurements, try different fabrics, use different paint colours and patterns. Make these projects yours, and put your stamp on them.

Now go and get messy and have fun! Explore your creative side and put your heart in your home.

Catherine

The Heart of the Home

Kitchen

Whether your kitchen is a galley, L-shaped or one-wall, it is safe to say that this is a hot spot of action in most homes. I know that in my house, the kitchen is the first place people go and congregate. It's where we have chats over mugs of tea, and the kitchen table doubles up as a doodle area when my niece and nephew visit.

Some of the most common pain points in our kitchens are outdated cabinets and counters, lack of storage or space, and clutter. Tackling these issues can help make the kitchen more functional, appealing and comfortable.

Kitchen renovations are expensive, and even more so right now, with the costs of materials and labour rising. In this section, I want to share some practical and pretty projects that warm up your home's heart, whatever your budget.

Kitchen Revamp

The kitchen is the hardest-working room in the house, so it's no surprise that it can be the most expensive to renovate too. Over the years, I have been tackling jobs in my kitchen to create a functional, inviting space that gives me joy.

Back in 2013, when I purchased my home, all my money had gone on the deposit and fees, so I had to get creative and roll up my sleeves. Saving up for a big kitchen renovation can take time, but there are plenty of ways you can revamp and refresh on a budget.

Before tackling a DIY project, weigh up the pros and cons of each option and consider your DIY skills, the time it will take and the cost. You can also take your budget kitchen reno in stages, tackling one area at a time.

Kitchen cabinetry

Custom built-in cabinets are very on trend, but of course they are expensive as they are made by highly skilled tradespeople. Here are some ways you can upgrade your cabinets by yourself, whatever your home decor style.

- Paint existing cabinets with a pop of colour or a neutral tone. See our Painting Guide on page 201.
- Re-stain solid wood cabinets or sand them to create a lighter wood tone.
- Use a vinyl wrap to cover old cabinets (renter friendly!).
- Look on second-hand online sites for people selling old kitchen units. You can use old cabinets as the bones for your new kitchen.
- Upgrade a flat-pack kitchen with wood moulding and trim to create a custom look on a budget.
- If your cabinet boxes are in good condition, replace just the doors and drawer fronts to give the cabinets a new look.
- Open shelving can be a fun way to create an airy feel in your kitchen. Why not remove the upper cabinets and put in shelves instead?
- Replace the hardware. New handles and knobs are a simple way to upgrade your cabinets. Have fun mixing and matching.

Countertops

Countertops can have a significant impact on a kitchen. For almost a decade, I lived with a dark laminate countertop, which made the kitchen feel shady and small no matter what colour I painted my cabinets. So once I had the money, I replaced the countertop with a white one, and instantly my kitchen felt bigger.

As with everything, you can skimp or splurge here. If you have a smaller budget, go for materials like laminate, butcher's block and concrete. More expensive options are natural stone like granite, marble and soapstone; quartz is also a popular option made from stone and resin.

Here are my tips for picking the perfect budget countertop.

- Measure twice, buy once. Most laminate counters from DIY shops will come in a standard size. You may need to have it cut, or you might need a longer piece.
- Get a custom size. Some DIY stores and IKEA offer a service where you can order a custom-size counter for your kitchen. You can make an appointment and give your measurements to a specialist, who will create a bespoke counter.
- Installation. If you are confident with cutting and caulking, you can save money and replace your counters without calling in the experts. Depending on the size of the kitchen, this is a two-person job, so get a friend to help.
- My biggest counter-tip is to hire help where needed. While I am fairly confident with a drill and a silicone gun, when doing my own countertops, the weight was just too much and I didn't feel

comfortable doing it all myself, so I happily paid two lads to install it for me. As a price guide, mine cost around €650, which included the new white laminate counter and the cost of labour.

Backsplash

Changing up a backsplash is another great way to revamp your space. There are loads of options available, from mosaics to chicken-printed wall tiles, in all shapes and sizes. Tiling is a skill, but if you have the time and patience to learn, you could do this one yourself – or you can always call in a tradesperson to do it for you.

Here are some tips if you want to revamp your existing tiles on a budget.

- Tile paint: You can buy paint designed especially for covering ceramic and porcelain tiles. Depending on the brand, you may need to use a special primer first. Painting tiles is a budget- and time-friendly way to change up your old tiles, but bear in mind that the paint may deteriorate over time. See page 21 for some tips on tile painting.
- Peel-and-stick tiles: You'll find lots of peel-and-stick tiles online and in DIY shops – they're a great option if you're renting. When shopping for peel-and-stick, try a tester first, as some are better quality than others.
- Vinyl stickers: If you have a plain tile, you can add a simple pattern or print to the tile with vinyl stickers. You can purchase these online, or if you have a vinyl-cutting machine, you can create and cut your own.
- Most kitchen mess happens around the cooker and sink. You can save money by only tiling around these areas and using wipeable kitchen paint on the other backsplashes.
- A mirrored backsplash can give the illusion of more light and space. Get a piece of mirror cut to size and use a strong adhesive to stick it to the wall. Opt for an aged effect on the mirror if you want that rustic feel.

Swap out your sink and tap

My dream has always been to have a bright and airy cottage-style kitchen, but when I bought my house, the reality was a dark laminate kitchen with a stainless-steel sink full of limescale. So one of the first things I did was to buy a white ceramic sink and a new tap to upgrade my plate-washing space.

Nowadays, you can get different coloured sinks and taps to suit your style. Black taps and basins have become popular, as well as gold. If you are happy with the rest of your kitchen and want a mini upgrade, swapping out your sink, taps and hardware can make a big difference.

Kitchen furniture

Most kitchen tables double up as a homework hot spot or a craft table, or even a home office. Kitchen and dining tables can be expensive, but you can get excellent second-hand items online that you can paint or stain to suit.

I bought a solid-wood round kitchen table and four chairs on a second-hand site for €50. I have had it for about eight years, so it has served me well. Over the years, it has been painted white, stripped back to wood and whitewashed, and I have sanded and re-sealed the tabletop as needed.

How to shop online like a pro:

- Set a search alert for the type of furniture or item you want, to help you stay away from things you do not need.
- Be strict with measurements. Having a table that is too large for your kitchen is a common mistake, and it can make the room feel smaller and uncomfortable.
- Check items for damage and factor the cost of repairs into your budget. A solid-wood table is worth salvaging, and minor repairs to the wood shouldn't be too dear. However, if you are a beginner upcycler, try to avoid any items that have woodworm or water damage.
- Flat pack hack! The internet is buzzing with furniture hacks for flat-pack items. For example, adding a countertop can turn an old flat-pack chest of drawers into a mini kitchen island.

Just like elsewhere in your home, you can also change up your kitchen flooring, lighting and wall colour. When planning your remodel, sit with your paint and material samples for a while until you are happy with them.

You don't have to rip your kitchen apart in one weekend (unless you really want to!). Instead, you can change it gradually, over time, to suit your budget and lifestyle.

Hand-painted Coasters

When picking a canvas for your artwork, a tile mightn't be the first thing that comes to mind. A few years back, I visited Sintra in Portugal and fell in love with all the hand-painted ceramics at the markets. The streets of Portugal were also full of decorative tiles, and I loved how dainty they looked and how they added charm and character.

Let me share an easy way to paint on a tile. A painted tile or coaster would make a cute present, and it's a lovely project to do with younger artists. You can pick up tile samples in most hardware stores or online, or look on second-hand sites for any free leftover or reclaimed tiles. A tile with a smooth, glossy surface is best.

What you need

A blank tile
Water and vinegar in a spray bottle, or dish soap
Ceramic paint suitable for porcelain and glass
An artist's palette
Paintbrushes
Stencil (optional)
Cork dots or cork base

- Prep the tile by cleaning the surface with either a water and vinegar spray or warm, soapy water to remove any grime before painting.
- Pour a small amount of paint onto your artist's palette and mix your colours as desired.
- If using a stencil, you can tape it to the tile or hold it firmly as you apply the paint, as this will stop the paint from bleeding underneath. You'll notice that the consistency of ceramic paint is a bit different to other paints. It's similar to acrylic, but the brushstrokes might feel different when painting on the

porcelain tile rather than a canvas.

- Have fun painting and figuring out what brushstrokes work for you. For example, on my flower, I like layering the paint thicker around the head and stem and then lighter around the base to create grass.

- Don't worry if you have any bleeding from a stencil, as you can wipe this away with a Q-tip or tissue paper or blend it with your brush. I like using stencils as a guide, as I have yet to perfect my flower painting skills!

- If you make a mistake while the paint is touch dry, you can use a window scraper and some water and vinegar to gently scrape the design away.

- Allow the paint to dry for twenty-four hours before baking, and avoid washing for twenty-four hours after that.

- Depending on the paint you use (see instructions on the pack), oven-bake your tile for around thirty minutes at 140°C (280°F). Carefully remove the tile from the oven using oven mitts and allow it to cool down.

- Gently hand wash your tile in warm, soapy water. Avoid soaking it, and don't pop it in a dishwasher.

- To turn your tile into a coaster, apply your cork dots to each corner of the base. Most cork dots come pre-glued, but if not, use some glue to stick them.

- It's not recommended to paint surfaces used for food and drink, so use your lovely painted tiles for decoration only. You could also modify this idea and paint on ceramic plates, teacups or a glass coaster.

Easy Sew Curtain

A fabric curtain is easy to make and a great way to hide things! If you don't want visitors to see a washing machine or a cluttered corner of the kitchen, or if you want to add curtains to an upcycled piece of furniture, this one's for you.

I used an old bedsheet to make a curtain for my kitchen nook (see photos on page 26) and a spare piece of thick cotton for my cabinet curtain (opposite). If you're a beginner, lightweight cotton or polycotton is the easiest to work with. Oilcloth is another option; it is wipeable, hard-wearing and durable for the kitchen.

If you're unfamiliar with any of the language in the sewing projects, check out the Sewing Terminology guide on page 198.

What you need

Cotton or polycotton fabric
Tape measure
Fabric marker
Fabric scissors
Sewing pins
Iron
Sewing machine
A curtain wire cord set with hook and eye

- Begin by measuring the width of the area you want to cover and add 2 in (5 cm) for the hem at either side.
- Measure the length of the area and add 4 in (10 cm). The extra inches will create a pocket for the curtain rod at the top.
- Use a tape measure and fabric marker to transfer your measurements onto your fabric, then cut the fabric to size with a sharp pair of fabric scissors.
- Create a hem on both sides of the fabric curtain first. To create a hem, iron the raw edge of the fabric over ⅕ in (½ cm) and press with your iron, then fold over again by ⅕ in (½ cm) and press. Use sewing pins to secure it in place. Then, using your sewing machine, sew a straight line of stitching down the hem to secure it in place.
- After hemming the sides, let's create a pocket for the cord. On the top of the fabric, fold over the raw

edge of the material by ⅕ in (½ cm) and press. Next, fold the cloth over by 1½ in (4 cm) and press. Finally, use sewing pins to pin the folded edge in place.

- When stitching the tunnel, the line of straight stitching should be approximately 1½ in (4 cm) from the edge of the fabric to allow room for the cord to go through. This is unlike sewing a regular hem, where you sew closer to the edge. You can adjust the measurements for the tunnel depending on how thick a cord you use. Take my measurements as a guide and tweak as needed.

- Your last piece of sewing will be for the bottom hem. Before sewing the bottom hem, I like to take the curtain to where it will go and check the final measurements. Then, you can adjust the hem and make it longer or shorter. Follow the same steps for the bottom hem as for those on the sides.

- Thread the curtain cord through the tunnel. You can trim most curtain cords with a wire cutter. Your cord will come with tiny screws and hooks. Screw the hooks into the two ends of the curtain rod and screw the other two into the area you are hanging.

- When creating curtains for a cabinet, I followed the steps above but did it twice to make two curtains. While you can add fabric panels to furniture with a staple or glue gun, I prefer this way. It's easier to remove and wash, and I can also swap the fabric curtains if I want to change the cabinet in the future.

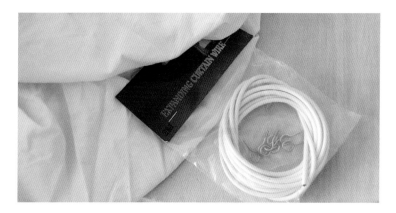

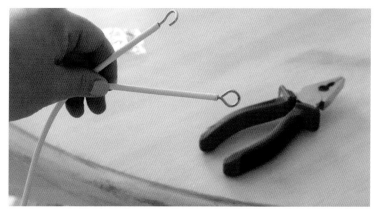

Eco Cleaning Products

Many years back, I decluttered my cleaning cupboard, which was full to the brim with the contents of the supermarket cleaning aisle. I had a bottle for this and two more for that. However, after suffering from migraines, I decided to cut down on the harsh smells and chemicals in my environment. The cleaning cupboard was one of the first places I made the switch. Changing to more eco-friendly and less toxic cleaners not only helped with my migraines but also saved me a lot of money over the years.

Now, I still buy certain things, like washing powder and bleach for the bathroom, but I no longer buy the newest scented spray and my cleaning cupboard isn't overflowing with plastic bottles. You don't have to gut your press completely, but if you want to save money and cut down on chemicals, then raid your kitchen cupboards for vinegar, baking soda and some lemons!

Vinegar

Not just for your fish and chips, vinegar is also a workhorse in the home for cleaning. You can buy large five-litre bottles of white (note: not malt) vinegar cheaply in most euro/pound/dollar stores and online, or pick up a smaller bottle in the supermarket for less than a euro.

For cleaning:

Grab a spray bottle and mix up 50/50 vinegar and distilled water. You can add a few drops of essential oil to ease the smell; for a 500 ml spray bottle, I add 15-20 drops of essential oil. Lemon is my favourite, but sometimes in winter I will add apple and cinnamon for a cosy scent. Note that some essential oils can be toxic to pets, so do some research or reach out to your vet for advice.

This vinegar/water spray is the one I use the most at home. It is excellent for cutting through bathroom watermarks, cleaning windows, or as an all-around surface spray. I also use it when dusting down skirting boards, window frames, etc. You should avoid using vinegar on porous surfaces like marble, granite or certain types of stone, as it can cause damage.

For smells:

Now, I know what you're thinking … 'Will my house not smell like vinegar?' Fear not: the smell disappears quickly, especially when used on a hard surface. I find that once it has dried, the scent is

gone in at most thirty minutes – a little longer on soft furnishings and fabrics.

Vinegar is known for being a natural deodoriser, and as it evaporates, it removes neutralised molecules and leaves no scent. If you have a stale odour in a room, leave a small bowl of vinegar in a corner. Or have you cooked something stinky in the kitchen? Boil a small pot with 50/50 water and vinegar and let it simmer for a few minutes to help eliminate strong cooking odours.

As a fabric softener:

You can also swap vinegar for shop-bought fabric softeners, as it leaves your clothes fresh and soft. Add ¼ cup of white vinegar to the fabric softener dispenser of your washing machine when washing your clothes. It also prevents static: lint and pet hair are less likely to cling to your clothing.

Speaking of pet hair, an internet hack I stumbled across is to use a rubber cleaning glove to wipe away pet hair from fabric surfaces. I find this helpful when running out the door and wiping away cat hair from my jumper or leggings!

For limescale:

If, like me, you live in a hard-water area, you are probably familiar with pesky limescale on your taps in the kitchen and bathroom. Well, before whipping out the harsh limescale cleaners, give vinegar a try. I like to pour white vinegar directly onto a cloth and wipe around the surface of my taps. For more stubborn limescale, I wrap the cloth around the tap for thirty minutes and rinse away. With shower heads, you can soak them for thirty minutes in a bowl or bucket of a 50/50 vinegar-to-water solution to remove limescale.

Lemon juice is another fantastic limescale remover; you can use it like above. If you have coloured taps, make sure to test an area first – this goes for shop-bought cleaners too.

Noisy kettle? Me too! It might be due to a limescale build-up. To descale a kettle, fill it up with equal parts vinegar and water. Let it soak for an hour, then boil and rinse your kettle thoroughly. (The most challenging part of this job is lasting an hour without a cup of tea!)

Continue the natural theme in your home with some beautiful scents! Find out how to make reed room diffusers on page 40 and pretty lavender pouches on page 110.

Bicarbonate of soda

Also known as baking soda and not to be confused with baking powder, bicarb is another safe, natural and effective alternative to commercial cleaning products and something that might already be lurking in the back of your cupboard.

For ovens:

Bicarbonate of soda is a great degreaser and odour eliminator. To clean your oven, mix the bicarbonate of soda with water to create a paste, then spread it all over the inside of your oven. Let it sit for a few hours (or overnight), then wipe it away with a damp cloth, or use a scraper or wire wool (and some elbow grease!) to really get in there. I tried mixing vinegar with bicarb but found it wasn't as effective. You get this satisfying fizzing and bubbling when the two mix, but they cancel each other out and turn to salty water. Creating a paste with water is more effective.

Oven tip! Did you know you can easily remove your oven door? Most models will have a clip on the bottom sides that you can flick and lift off the door, making it really easy to get inside to scrub and rinse.

For carpets:

Need to refresh a rug or revive the carpet? Sprinkle some bicarbonate of soda, let it sit for a few hours, then hoover it up for a fresh, clean scent.

In the bathroom:

Like vinegar, bicarb can be used to clean sinks, toilets and bathtubs. I like to mix it with water to create a paste, bung it on a sponge or cloth, scrub my ceramic areas, and then rinse away.

On clothes:

Want to brighten white clothing? Add a cup of bicarbonate of soda to your laundry to help brighten whites and remove odours.

Mini Kitchen Pantry

Storage is a common problem in most kitchens. Sometimes more is needed, but sometimes we just need to learn how to use the space properly. I am guilty of having the kitchen drawer of doom and the overflowing press full of half-empty bags of food!

Using shelves or upcycled cabinets is a great way to add more storage to a bare wall. It can free up space elsewhere and help you feel more organised.

I decided to create this mini pantry from an old shelf. My cabinets are now less jam-packed, and I made something practical but also pretty in my kitchen.

When thrifting or searching for suitable second-hand pieces online, look for old kitchen plate racks and wall-mounted kitchen shelves. You can sand, paint or stain pieces to suit your style and even remove spindles to make your storage containers fit your space.

What you need

A stud finder (for plasterboard/drywall; see note below)
An old shelf
Spirit level
Pencil
A drill
Screws
Wall fixing / wall plugs (see note below)

You can get special drywall anchors if you cannot locate studs or if the studs are not where you want to hang the shelf. These are commonly known as Molly bolts or hollow wall anchors.

You will need different fixings for different types of walls. For example, if you are hanging a shelf on plasterboard, it will require different hardware than if you are hanging it on a masonry wall. In the hardware shop, screws and fixings are typically sorted by project type, such as masonry or drywall. The screw packets also include detailed information about where to use the screws and fixings. Now, let's hang your shelf!

- If drilling into plasterboard, locate the studs in the wall where you want to hang the shelf; you can use a stud finder or tap on the wall and listen for a solid sound. See note above.
- Hold the shelf in place on the wall. Use your spirit level to make sure it is level and centred. Use a

pencil to mark the location of the holes on the wall.

- Use your drill to drill holes into your markings on the wall, making sure they are deep enough to insert the screws.

- Insert a wall plug into the hole (or a Molly bolt if it is drywall; see note on page 33). Hold the shelf in place again and insert the screws into the holes. Tighten the screws until the shelf is secure.

- I use glass storage jars to store the likes of pasta, rice and coffee and tea. You can pick up these glass containers in various sizes online or in most home decor shops. When picking glass jars, measure the size before buying them to ensure they will be manageable and won't fall off your shelf. I stuck a small, reusable label on the base of each jar for the best-before dates.

When unpacking my food shopping, I remove the excess wrapping before storing items. For example, my six-pack of King crisps come out of their bag and into a basket in the naughty drawer. Removing the extra packaging before storing helps keep drawers and presses less cluttered and overwhelming.

Pretty Tiled Tray

I fell in love with these adorable floral tiles a few years ago, but unfortunately, I didn't have any-where for them on my walls. So I decided to experiment with a tiled wooden tray. That was back in 2018, and my skills have improved slightly since then!

I will share two ways to create a tiled tray. You can use a tray you have already, in which case you'll skip the first set of instructions. But if you feel like flexing your woodworking skills with a straightforward project, read on …

Note: For projects like these where you need to be precise, it's best to measure in millimetres, so I haven't included inches in the measurements.

What you need

MDF board
Measuring tape and ruler (or T-square) and pencil
Wood clamps
Safety mask and goggles
Circular saw
2 x 1-inch wood
Hand saw and mitre box
Wood glue, tack nails (I used 16 mm), hammer
★ Paint/stain (optional)
★ Decorative tiles
★ Serving tray
★ Adhesive
★ Grout, smoothing tool and damp rags

★ if you are using an existing tray, you only need items marked with an asterisk

To make the wooden tray:

• Cut MDF base to 45.5 x 35.5 cm. I used a scrap piece of MDF that was 9 mm thick, but you can use thicker wood too. You could also use reclaimed wood for the base. When cutting your MDF base, measure and mark with a pencil. I find it easier to get a precise measurement with a T-square than a measuring tape and ruler, but use what you have in your crafty stash. I used a circular saw to cut my MDF, but you can also use a hand saw. Use woodworking clamps to clamp the wood to a strong

surface before cutting and be sure to wear your mask and goggles.

- Next, you'll cut your 2 x 1 wood. Cut two pieces 45.5 cm long and two pieces 35.5 cm long. I cut each end at a 45-degree angle using a mitre box and saw. Mitres can be confusing if you're a beginner, so you can cut these straight if you prefer.

- Apply a bead of wood glue to the 2 x 1's and firmly place them onto the base. Clamp the wood in place and allow the glue to dry.

- Hammer in some tack nails to secure the base to the side pieces. Adding some nails will help the tray take the weight, as the tiles can be heavy. Ensure your nails are fully hammered into the wood to avoid scratching your table.

To tile the wooden tray:

- You can choose to paint or stain your tray to suit your style – best to do this before tiling. For tips on painting, check out page 201. I am doing a feminine and floral tray here, but you could use retro tiles and create a bougie tray that would look fab at a home bar or drinks corner.

- Before tiling, arrange your decorative tiles in your favourite pattern. Rearrange and move things around until you are satisfied.

- You can pick up small pots of tile adhesive and grout in most hardware stores, or use strong glue to adhere the tiles to the base. Just check that the glue is suitable for ceramic and wood.

- If you are using a serving tray that you didn't make, check that it can hold the weight of the tiles before adding, and if it's a second-hand tray, look for any damage to the base before using it.

- Smooth out your adhesive and place your tiles firmly on the base. Allow the adhesive to dry thoroughly, which can take up to twenty-four hours, depending on the temperature in your home.

- I didn't use tile spacers; instead, I used a ruler tip to check that they were even as I placed them.

- Once the tiles are fully dry, it is time to grout them. This is the fun part, kind of like icing a cake. Add grout to the gaps between the tiles and smooth it using a smoothing tool (an old bank card would work too). Wipe away any excess grout with a damp cloth and allow it to dry for twenty-four hours.

- The next day, polish the tiles and remove any remaining grout with a damp cloth.

Down Time

Living Room

When I imagine my dream living room, it's a cosy and inviting space that allows me to unwind after a long day. While the kitchen is the heart of the home, the living room is a social hub with a special charm. There is nothing quite like settling down in the evening with a steaming mug of tea, lighting a candle and enjoying a box set marathon before a roaring fire.

Living rooms can often be dual spaces, with many having work-from-home nooks. Even the couch sometimes becomes a 'soft office' for me. Pain points here can be lack of storage, character and design. You want your living room to look pretty but also be functional for you and your family.

In this section, I will share my DIY and decor tips to help you create a living space that suits your personal taste and enhances your home's functionality and flow. From wallpapering like a pro to adding some DIY art, let's dive in and get inspired.

DIY Room Diffuser

Creating your own diffuser is a great way to add a subtle scent to a room. They are straightforward to make, and you might already have the supplies sitting in your kitchen cupboards or crafty stash.

What is a reed diffuser, I hear you ask? It is a type of room diffuser that uses reeds or sticks to absorb and disperse essential oils. The reeds are placed in a container filled with oil, and the oil travels up the reeds, releasing the scent into the air.

You might have stumbled across these in the candle section of your favourite store and noticed their hefty price tag. So, gather your supplies and let's make some of our own!

What you need

Ceramic or glass vase
Measuring jug
Sweet almond oil
Essential oils of your choice
Reed diffuser sticks or bamboo sticks

- Choose a glass or ceramic vase with a narrow top opening to slow down evaporation. Check its capacity by pouring in water from a measuring jug, then dry thoroughly.
- When picking a base oil, choose one that is lightweight. I used sweet almond oil here, but from searching online, I know safflower, coconut and sunflower oil are also popular.
- Pour your sweet almond oil into a measuring jug. Add 8–10 drops of essential oils per 100 ml of sweet almond oil and stir well. I wanted an autumn scent, so I went for spiced apple and cinnamon. Geranium is lovely for spring, as are lavender and lemongrass. Add more essential oils for a stronger scent.
- Pour your mixture into your chosen vase and insert eight or ten reed diffuser sticks. I didn't have any reed sticks, but I did have a massive bag of bamboo sticks in my craft stash, so I cut off their sharp edges and stuck them inside. Just give the reeds or skewers a little flip after an hour or when they're halfway wet.
- To reinvigorate the scent, flip the reeds every other day and replace the oil mixture once a month.
- These diffusers are quick to make, great for presents, and could even be a DIY wedding favour. I love that you can adjust the intensity of the fragrance. I mention on page 27 that certain smells cause me migraines. So, by creating my own scent, I have control over what is released into the air in my home.

Circle Mirrors

Circular mirrors are all the rage, and for good reason! They can be hung individually, grouped together, or you can do different sizes and mix them up. In this project, I will show you how to transform a gift box into a mini circular mirror that will make a stylish addition to any room.

You can purchase small, light mirrors from most craft shops or online. They come in various sizes and are generally inexpensive – I paid €5 for a pack of three 15 cm mirrors. As for the paint, chalk or acrylic will look great, and tester pots are perfect.

Feel free to get creative! You could do a square mirror instead of round. And if painting isn't your thing, try covering the lid with a beautiful fabric.

What you need

A gift box
Measuring tape
Self-adhesive mirrors
An old belt or strap
Picture frame hangers
Hot glue gun and glue sticks
Paint and brushes

- Use a measuring tape to measure the box's circumference and pick a mirror that will sit comfortably inside. I made three mirrors here, using gift box lids and bases.
- Begin by painting your lid. Apply two coats and allow the paint to dry (follow instructions on tin).
- Once the paint is fully dry, apply hot glue to the back of the mirror and firmly place it inside the lid. Most craft mirrors have a self-adhesive backing, but it's best to add an extra bit of glue for security.
- To add a strap (I used an old belt for one of mine), find the mid point of each side, apply hot glue and firmly fix each end of the strap to the box. Once the glue sets, check that the strap is strong enough to hold the weight. If you're using a particularly big and heavy mirror, screw in the belt strap instead, as hot glue may not be strong enough and we don't want seven years of bad luck if your mirror falls.
- If you don't want a strap, add a picture frame hanger to the back instead before hanging on the wall.
- Mirrors can work wonders in a room, reflecting light and adding a touch of whimsy. Even the dullest corner can be transformed into a bright and inviting spot with this simple addition!

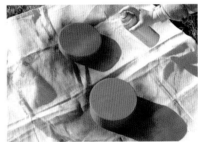

Framing Memories

One of my favourite things to do while travelling is to take photos. However, I am guilty of having a camera roll with thousands of photos and not one picture on display in my home!

Photos have a way of bringing you right back to a time and place, in the same way a scent or taste can. While doing this project, I was giddy with excitement when my canvases arrived. I even texted my friend Rachel and said, 'Remember when we went to Sorrento? That's where this picture was taken!' I had a little moment of nostalgia and a warm feeling of gratitude and joy when I looked back on it.

Photography is also a way to flex your creative muscle, and you don't need fancy gear to get started – just your phone! For me, snapping pictures helps me be more mindful and aware of the beauty around me. Especially when life is hectic, I feel calmer if I can be still and look for small moments of beauty throughout the day.

What you need

Your favourite photos printed onto canvas
Measuring tape and pencil
Wood trim (see notes below)
Safety goggles and gloves
Mitre saw, or mitre box and hand saw
Wood stain
Sponges and cloths
Clear varnish or wax
Wood glue
Woodworking clamps

- Send your favourite photos to a local printing service or online shop. I was able to get my photos printed on canvas for around €15 each, but prices will vary depending on the size you want.
- Begin by measuring the sides of your canvas. The canvases I ordered were 12 x 16 in, but in millimetres, they were exactly 303 x 404 mm. Take your time when measuring wood; measure in mm for a more accurate cut.
- For my trim, I used a thin piece of wood moulding that had a curved edge, but you can use thicker wood or pieces left over from previous projects.

- This project is a great way to practise your mitre corners and build up your confidence with cutting and measuring. Use a tape measure and pencil to mark your measurements onto your wood. Pop on your safety goggles and gloves.

- When cutting a mitre, the long edge is the outer or longer side of the wood, and the short edge is the inner or shorter side. When measuring and cutting, you mark the outside or longer edge of the wood with a pencil and cut into the wood, ensuring that the other edge is shorter. This way, when you combine the pieces, they fit perfectly at a 45-degree angle, creating a neat corner.

- Cut both ends of a piece at a 45-degree angle. If you use a thin wood, it's better to use a hand saw and a mitre box, as you will have more control over the cut. Sometimes, the power of a mitre saw can cause splinters in thin wood. I like to cut a side piece first, check if it needs any adjustments, and then use that piece as my guide for cutting the other pieces on that frame.

- Once the wood is cut, you can either paint or stain it, or if you like the grain of the wood, leave it bare and seal it with some wax or varnish.

- Attaching the wood to the canvas can be tricky, but using wood glue will give you more time to line up the wood compared to a quick-drying glue.

- Apply a bead of glue to the wood and press it to the side of the canvas, using a clamp to secure it in place. Attach all four sides to the canvas and allow the glue to dry. If you have slight gaps, you can cheat a little: take some of the wood shavings from cutting and mix them into a paste with wood glue, and you can use it as a bit of DIY wood filler. Sand your filler smooth and stain/paint over to hide.

- Remove the clamps once the wood is dry, then hang and enjoy your beautifully framed memories.

Stylish Wood Staining

During the spring, while I was writing this book, I started doing woodwork classes at my local school and I made this stool (see photo on next page), which I use as a side table in my living room. While my woodwork skills still need practice, I was so pleased with how it turned out, and I wanted to show off the dovetail joints that I had painstakingly chiselled out.

Over the years, I have mainly used paint to transform old pieces of furniture. Any sign of orange pine and my paintbrush comes out! But I am also a fan of the grain and detail within natural wood, and I love mixing and matching different pieces in my home. Wood stain doesn't have to be 1990s orange – you can layer different shades to get the desired effect.

If you have an old piece of wooden furniture (or even a new one), wood stain and tinted waxes can be a great way to get a rustic look and give it some character.

If you need to strip a piece of furniture and remove the old paint first, check out the guide on page 204.

What you need

Wooden furniture
Sandpaper (medium and fine grit)
Lint-free cloth
Stirring stick
Gloves
Wood stain or gel
Sponge or brush
Clear topcoat (wax or varnish)

- Prepping wood for staining is more detailed than prepping for paint. When preparing a piece of furniture for paint, I lightly scuff/key it to help the paint adhere. However, when staining wood, you need to get it as smooth as possible or the stain will highlight imperfections. For example, I had a few marks on my wood from using an electric sander; you couldn't see them before staining, but they showed up once stained. So, I sanded that area once the stain had dried and applied a second coat. Dried wood glue can also show up when you apply stain, so take some extra time to sand off any excess wood glue that may have bled through.

- Start with medium grit sandpaper (100–150 grit) to remove any marks or wood glue, and then smooth with some fine grit paper (180 grit +). Wipe away any excess dust with a cloth or hoover.

- Give your wood stain a good stir, and test the stain on a less visible area first to check if it's the colour you want. Some wood stain brands can have a longer re-coat time compared to water-based paints, so you may need to wait until the next day to apply a second coat (check the tin for info).

- If you are new to staining, wood stain gels can be easier to work with and less watery. I find I have more control over them and get less patchiness.

- I prefer to use a sponge to apply the wood stain in the direction of the grain and smooth it into the wood, then I wipe away any excess with my lint-free cloth. For my ladies who use fake tan, wood staining is similar!

- Allow to dry thoroughly then apply a second coat. You can layer different shades of stain to get different effects. For example, you can use a darker stain to create shadows or emphasise the wood's knots.

- Lightly sand between coats, especially if you've patchy or dripping areas.

- To seal your wood, you can use wax or varnish, or some stains are self-sealing. Just like paint finishes, you can get varnishes and oils in matt, satin and gloss finish.

- If you opt to seal your piece with a varnish or lacquer, I always recommend water-based clear varnish, as I know from experience that the oil-based ones can go yellow over time. Use a sponge roller and tray to apply an even coat of varnish and avoid brush strokes.

- As you can see from my table, I decided to add some white hard wax oil for a rustic look. Some brands offer coloured and tinted waxes and hard wax oils that will seal the wood and give a coloured effect. White wax or lime wax gives a shabby chic look, and you can use this on light or dark wood.

- Varnish and wax, just like paint, will have a cure time, so even if the piece seems dry, take extra care for a few more days. No hot mugs of tea on a freshly waxed surface – a lesson I learnt the hard way!

Wallpaper Like a Pro!

Wallpaper is a fun way to inject a room with character, bringing in pattern, texture and personality. As a kid, I remember the 1980s floral wallpaper in my nanna's living room. Back then, it seemed like every inch of a room was covered in paper, with a charming floral border strip along the middle. Nowadays, wallpaper has evolved, offering endless design possibilities for creating feature walls or adding a touch of flair to a nook in your home.

As I was writing this book, I took on a few wallpapering projects myself. Some I tackled solo, and others, I had a helping hand. If it's your first time, consider persuading a friend to join you, as it can be fiddly. But don't worry – with a little patience, we'll soon have you wallpapering like a pro.

What you need

Wallpaper
Filler and sandpaper (if needed)
Cloth
Spirit level
Measuring tape
Pencil
A wallpaper table or a flat surface
Wallpaper paste
Wallpaper brush
Utility knife or wallpaper scissors
A sponge and a bucket of water

Get things rolling

When picking wallpaper, I noticed most options were 'paste the wall'. So instead of pasting the paper on a table before hanging it, you paste the wall and then hang the wallpaper directly on. I found these easier to use and less messy.

To work out how many rolls you need, measure the height and width of the wall you plan to paper. If your wallpaper has a pattern with a repeat (the vertical distance between where the pattern starts and repeats itself), keep this in mind when measuring up. You'll need more wallpaper if it has a large repeat, to make sure it matches and lines up correctly.

You'll find the width and length on the wallpaper roll, as well as the repeat. If shopping online, check this info in the description box before buying.

Here is a formula to help you work out how many rolls you need:

(Wall width) ÷ (roll width) x (wall height + pattern repeat) = number of rolls

Some online wallpaper shops have a calculator that will do the sums for you.

It's always a good idea to add an extra roll to your total count in case of mishaps or repairs. You can use leftover wallpaper for other projects around the house. (Hands up who had wallpapered schoolbooks back in the 1990s!)

Prep

Before adding wallpaper to the wall, prepare the surface. (See page 54 to find out how to strip old wallpaper.) Patch holes or cracks with some filler, smooth any bumps with sandpaper, and wipe down the wall with a damp cloth to remove dust and dirt.

Plan

If you have a simple wallpaper that doesn't have an intricate design, start your first strip in a less noticeable area in your room, for example behind a door. If the pattern is bold, place the first strip in the centre of the room's focal point and work outwards, for example at a chimney breast.

When papering my chimney breast, I placed the first strip of wallpaper in the centre. I got lucky as there was a pencil mark from the previous wallpaper, so I could use that as a guide. Otherwise find the centre of the area, and use a spirit level and pencil to mark a line to use as a guide for placing the first strip.

Hang

Measure and trim the wallpaper before applying any paste. Measure the height of your wall, from the skirting board to the ceiling, and add a few inches to allow for trimming. Roll out your wallpaper on a clean, flat surface with the pattern side down. Use a measuring tape to mark the length of your wall on the back of the wallpaper and cut a straight edge.

Apply the wallpaper paste to either the back of the paper or the wall (check your wallpaper sleeve to see if your roll is 'paste the wall' or 'paste the paper').

Starting at the top of the wall, carefully position your wallpaper strip against it and use a spirit level to check it is straight. (I am someone who likes to eyeball things, but sometimes walls – especially in old houses – might not be straight!) Get the first strip perfect before putting up the next one.

When you are happy with the strip, use your wallpaper brush or sponge to gently press the wallpaper onto the wall, working from the centre outwards. Smooth the paper from top to bottom, ensuring that there are no bubbles or wrinkles.

Use a utility knife or wallpaper scissors to trim off the excess paper at the top and bottom of the wall. I like to fold the paper against the edge of the skirting board or ceiling before cutting; I smooth the fold with my thumb to get the line and then cut with a blade or scissors. I sometimes find my utility blade can tear the paper, so take your time when cutting to avoid a jagged edge.

Repeat the above steps for each wallpaper strip, ensuring the edges line up neatly.

After you've hung all the wallpaper strips, use a damp sponge to clean off any excess paste from the surface, rinsing the sponge frequently in water to keep it clean.

Awkward angles

If you encounter a difficult angle such as a curve or a corner, cut the strip of paper roughly to size and use your finger to roughly mark the curve onto the paper. Then use your utility knife or wallpaper scissors to carefully cut the excess wallpaper, following the shape of the curve.

For example, I had a curved window in my niece's bedroom. I cut the strip at the height I needed

and hung it on the wall. Then I used my finger to trace the curved window shape onto the paper before cutting the line with my scissors. You can also create a template from brown paper if the angle is really tricky. Use the template to trace the shape onto your wallpaper.

Here are my tips for going around electrical sockets:

- Begin by turning off the power at the fuse box. Then, with the wallpaper on the wall, feel through the wallpaper to locate the corners of the plug socket.
- Diagonally cut slits from the middle of the socket to each corner, allowing you to manoeuvre the wallpaper around the socket. Next, fold back the four triangular flaps created by the slits and trim them so that about 10 mm sticks out from the wall.
- Unscrew the faceplate of the socket, fold down the 10 mm flaps firmly against the wall, and brush them in well. Finally, screw the faceplate back on. If you notice any slits extending past the socket, don't worry, as they won't be noticeable when dry.

Steps for stripping wallpaper

While it might be tempting to wallpaper over old wallpaper, it is not recommended! You risk poor adhesion, an uneven surface, moisture issues, difficulty in removal … and it can limit the lifespan of your lovely wallpaper.

As a kid, I remember helping strip layers of textured wallpaper from my nanna's living room. You know the wallpaper that had the little grains of wood chip? Thankfully the job is easier these days!

The old school method:

Start by removing any wallpaper borders or trim, then score the wallpaper surface using a scoring tool or sandpaper to create small perforations.

Apply a wallpaper stripping solution or hot water and fabric softener to the wallpaper surface. A spray bottle is perfect for spraying the solution onto the wall. Let the solution soak into the paper for ten to twenty minutes to loosen the adhesive. Then use a wallpaper scraper to gently peel off the softened wallpaper, starting from a corner or an edge. Work your way across the wall.

Once all the paper is removed, wipe down the wall with a cloth to remove any remaining adhesive and check for any damage you may need to repair before applying the new wallpaper.

Steamer (my favourite):

If you have lots of wallpaper to strip or have many layers, then renting, borrowing or buying a wallpaper steamer might save you some time and effort. The job is still messy, but it is an excellent tool for lifting stubborn old paper. I used a steamer for my fireplace (see photos opposite).

Fill the steamer with water and allow it to heat up, then hold the steamer plate against a section of the wallpaper for a few seconds to steam the adhesive. Get your wallpaper scraper and lift the softened wallpaper gently. Continue steaming and scraping until all the wallpaper is removed.

When using the steamer, take extra care not to burn yourself or slip on water, as I find it can cause some water droplets to leak. Also, take care not to damage the surface of the wall.

Chemical strippers:

In the hardware and DIY shops, you will find loads of wallpaper strippers and adhesive removers. Personally, I think you can save money and follow the first two methods – I don't think it's necessary to bring in the chemicals unless you have some really stubborn paper or many layers.

These strippers are simple to use and have detailed instructions on the back of the packet about how to use them.

Apply the stripper onto the wallpaper surface using a sponge, brush or spray bottle, then allow the solution to penetrate and dissolve the adhesive; the instructions will tell you how long to leave it on. Use your wallpaper scraper to peel off the loosened wallpaper, then clean the wall surface with water or mild detergent to remove any residue.

Wine Bottle Candles

Wine bottles make perfect candle holders, so hang on to your empties and let's recycle them into something new. You can also use larger alcohol bottles, but wine bottles are perfect if you're a beginner. Cutting glass might sound scary, but it's easier than you'd expect.

Candles are a fun way to add warm, cosy lighting to a room, making them great DIY gifts. In this project, we'll first make our wine bottle candle holders, and then I'll talk you through an easy way to make gorgeous homemade candles that are a perfect fit.

To make your candle holders, you need

Empty wine bottles
Safety goggles and gloves
A bottle cutter or a glass cutter
Sandpaper (medium and fine grit)

- Begin by cleaning your bottle and removing any labels. Leave your bottles to steep for a few minutes in warm, soapy water, and it should be easy to peel the old labels off.
- Pop on your safety gloves and use your bottle or glass cutter to score an even line around the middle of the wine bottle. I like to use a bottle cutter as it holds the bottle in place as I slowly turn it to score. You can pick up a bottle cutter online or in craft shops for around €20.
- Try to cut the score line slowly, evenly and only once, as repeatedly going over the score line can cause the glass to break unevenly.
- Take the bottle and lay it in the sink. Pour boiling water along the score line, followed by cold water. The glass will contract, and the bottle will split in two. Some bottles have thicker glass so you may need to pour the boiling/cold water twice or three times before it separates.
- Have some extra bottles on hand for practising. While cutting bottles is surprisingly easy, it did take me a few tries to perfect the technique of getting a clean break.
- Use sandpaper to smooth out the edge of the glass. Begin with medium grit paper and sand the edge smoothly. Then, work up to fine grit sandpaper to get it extra smooth.

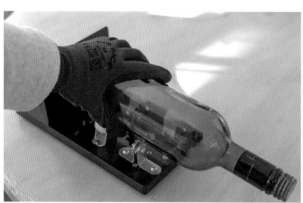

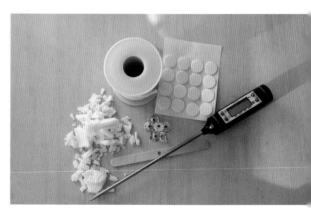

To make your candles, you need

Candle wax of your choice
A metal wax melting pot
Metal stirring spoon
Thermometer
Essential oil (optional)
Double-sided sticker or glue dots
Candle wicks
Lollipop sticks or chopsticks

- You can pick up a candle-making kit online or in a craft shop, with everything you need to create candles at home. If you plan on making a lot, these are an excellent investment and range from €15 upwards.

- How much wax you melt will depend on the size of your glass container. I melted 500 g of wax for each of my candles – it is easy to melt more and top them up if you need to. Soy and beeswax are my favourite candle waxes.

- Add your wax to your melting pot and heat slowly on a stove until the wax melts into a liquid. Wax can quickly get very hot, so use your thermometer to check the temperature. (Note: Keep your pot, stirrer and thermometer for craft use only and do not reuse them for food prep in the kitchen.)

- If you are adding scent, the ideal temperature to add in the essential oils is between 85°C and 93°C (185°F and 200°F), depending on the type of wax you use. For 500 g of melted wax, I add 2–3 tablespoons (30–45 ml) of essential oils. Lavender is a relaxing scent all year round, and in autumn, I love to use apple and cinnamon blends.

- Use a glue dot to stick the wick to the base of the bottle. Then, use a lollipop stick or chopstick to keep the wick upright and centred during your pour. You will notice that I used two small wicks in my candle to avoid tunnelling.

- Slowly pour the wax into the container and allow the melted wax to set for a few hours. Before using, trim the wick to ¼ in (⅔ cm), as this will help your candle to burn correctly.

- The great thing about home candle-making is that you can refill the candle containers with a scent of your choice whenever they burn through, saving you money in the long run.

Wainscoting

Wall framing or wainscoting is an excellent way to spruce up a plain wall in your home or add character to a new build. This kind of decorative panelling is typically installed on the lower portion or three-quarters of a wall, but I went a step further and added decorative framing pieces to the top too.

On page 119 you'll find another project for board and batten panelling. That one, I found easier – wainscoting can be tricky. The hardest parts for me were figuring out the right size for the squares and cutting those mitred corners perfectly. But once I got the hang of it I was thrilled with the results, and my living room went from plain to pretty.

With a little patience and lots of 'measuring twice and cutting once', you can confidently tackle this at home. We're going to be using millimetres for our measurements again, as this gives a more precise cut. Read on for my top tips and the lessons I learned along the way.

What you need

Wood moulding pieces
Measuring tape and pencil
Spirit level
Masking tape
Mitre saw, or hand saw and mitre box
Safety goggles and gloves
Wall adhesive and cartridge gun
Tack nails and hammer (or a nail gun)
Decorators caulk and cartridge gun
Primer and paint

Buying your wood

Some hardware shops now offer wood panelling kits with the wood trim packaged for you; some are even pre-cut. If you are nervous about measurements, this may be an option. Or you can bring your measurements to a hardware store that offers a cutting service, purchase your wood in-store and have it cut to size.

I bought a panelling pack from a local seller, which included a large dado for the centre, a smaller dado, and lengths of moulding that I needed to cut to size to create the square frames. So even though I purchased a panelling pack, I still had to handle all the wood cutting and measurements myself. If you don't feel comfortable doing this, make sure to double-check if yours comes pre-cut. Also, try to get pre-primed pieces, as this will save time when it comes to painting.

I highly recommend renting or borrowing a mitre saw for this project. There are many pieces to cut and a mitre box and hand saw will tire you out, especially when using chunkier MDF pieces.

Measure & mark

Before putting the pieces onto the wall, I marked them out with a pencil and spirit level. I am happy I did, as I had already made a few mistakes. Marking the wall with painter's tape would also help you visualise how it will look when finished. You can use cardboard or a square piece of scrap wood to make a template when marking up.

I began by measuring up from the skirting board. It is common to position the dado rail 900 mm from the skirting board, but you can adjust this height depending on the height of your wall. To establish the top of the dado rail, I measured the distance from the skirting board up to 720 mm using a tape measure. Then I marked the same distance up from the skirting board at intervals around the room, connecting the marks to form a line. Using a spirit level helped ensure the line was level, and it came in handy as a ruler.

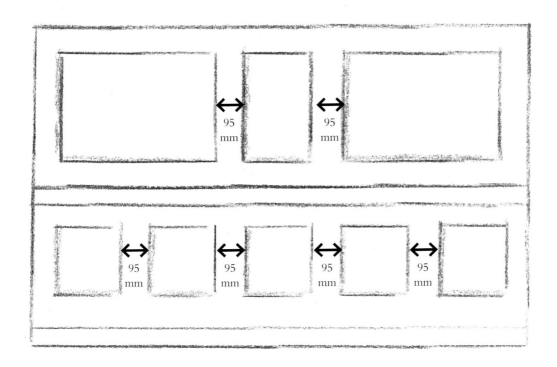

95 mm

95 mm

95 mm

95 mm

95 mm

95 mm

95 mm

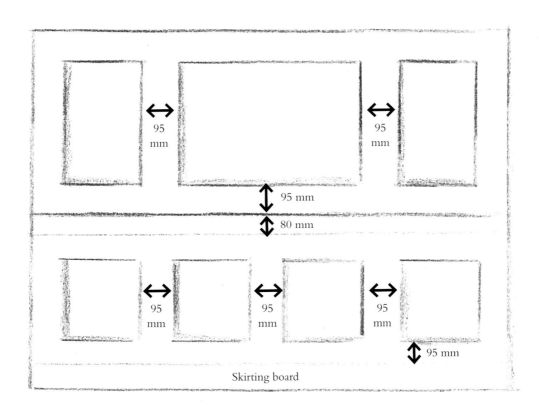

95 mm

95 mm

95 mm

95 mm

80 mm

95 mm

95 mm

95 mm

95 mm

Skirting board

Use a spirit level to check if your skirting and ceiling are level. If they are not (don't worry, this is quite common!), you may need to adjust the dado to get it level. This is why it's a really good idea to draw/tape the measurements on the wall first. Use your spirit level and your judgment, tweak the rail, and perfect it by eye. If I were to do this project again, I would spend more time planning and drawing to avoid mistakes.

Once you are happy with the first dado rail, you can draw on the sub rail (optional) or start drawing on the square frames. I made a handy block with measurements of my gaps in between (see diagram on previous page). I used a 95 mm gap between each square frame, but you can adjust this to be tighter to fit in more squares on your wall.

How many squares you put on your wall will depend on the width of your wall, the thickness of your wood and the gap you want between each square frame. Grab a sketch pad and work out how you want your wall to look. For example, on one wall, I went for two large and one smaller frame on top as I had an odd number of square frames on the bottom. I had a radiator on my other wall, so I used that as my middle and positioned the pieces around it.

Cutting and sticking

Once you are happy with the markings on the wall, it is time to start cutting.

Use a tape measure to mark your measurements onto your wood. See page 46 for details of how to cut mitres with a hand saw and mitre box (thinner wood) or a mitre saw (chunky wood).

Some of my most common mitre mistakes are:

- Cutting the pieces too short by measuring on the inner or shorter side, not the long side.
- Not aligning my saw blade correctly to the marked line, so my angle is slightly off. Nothing that some caulk or filler won't fix!

If you are new to cutting mitres, practise first on a smaller project. Mistakes are frustrating, but they are the best lessons.

Once you are measured and cut, you're on the home stretch. Apply a bead of adhesive to the back of the wood piece and firmly place it onto the wall, using your lines as your guide for positioning. Depending on your adhesive, you may have a ten- to twenty-minute window before it fully sets to tweak it. Use masking tape to secure the pieces in position if they are slipping, or tack the wood trim into place with a nail. I found I only had to use a nail gun on the heavier chair rail pieces – adhesive was enough for the others. (Before hammering a nail into the wall, make sure to check for pipes or electrical wires to avoid piercing them.)

Wipe away any excess adhesive that may bleed out from the wood; if this dries, it can look muddy when you go to paint over it later.

Painting time

When all the pieces are in place, caulk the inside and outside edges of the wood frames and any mitre corners with small gaps. Doing this will give your framing a polished, professional finish. I like to smooth the caulk with my finger and wipe away any excess with a damp cloth.

Now the fun part: apply your paint. If you have used bare wood, give it a coat of primer before starting your final topcoat.

You could do this project over a weekend, but be sure to take the time when planning the design. And if you're feeling wobbly, why not try it in a bedroom or another area that gets less traffic before doing the living room or dining room?

A Warm Welcome

Hall & Stairs

They're the first things that greet us when we arrive home, but unfortunately, hallways can easily become an obstacle course of shoes, bags and jackets. While I dream of having one of those fancy boot rooms you see online, my current reality is a tiny, narrow, L-shaped bungalow hallway. So, over the years, I have had to get creative and tackle some of those pain points in my space. The most common issue in this part of the house tends to be clutter, but it's also easy to overlook decor in these high-traffic spaces.

In this section, I will share some ideas that have helped me create an organised and bright space that fills me with calm when I return home.

Hallway Revamp

After a long day, there's nothing I like better than coming home, turning the key in the lock, and feeling the tension release from my body. The pitter-patter of paws greets me at the door, and all I want to do is pop my shoes off and put the slippers on.

Now, I might hold the record for the world's tiniest hallway. Having a small, awkward-shaped hall means I'm in a constant battle with the clutter, so I have to get creative with my hallway to keep it inviting and organised.

Here are some of my tips for creating an enticing entrance.

Furniture & storage

Although I have a small hallway, I managed to fit in a slim shoe storage cabinet, which I spruced up with a lick of paint. One of my pet peeves is having nowhere to kick off my shoes. If storage is an issue for you too, you can get many kinds of shoe cabinets that you can customise to your decor style. Flick to page 201 and check out the guide to painting furniture.

A narrow bench with storage can be both functional and pretty. Why not upholster a seat pad for an old blanket box and make a bench?

Baskets are another great way to stash random hallway items. I love pretty wicker baskets with lids, and they are great for hiding my scarves and slippers. You can use smaller storage boxes to hide keys and other little items.

Install hooks or pegs for hanging coats, hats or bags. If your hallway is relatively narrow, add coat hooks to the back of doors to keep your space clear.

Have you hidden storage? Many under-stair areas are blocked up, but there may be hidden storage potential there. You can get a professional out to assess, but I have seen these spaces transformed into mini offices, mini pantries and even pet houses.

If you have a larger hallway space, add a console table with vases and your favourite decorative items for that warm welcome.

Light it up

There never seem to be enough power outlets in the hall, but fear not: there are many cordless lamps on the market these days. Just pop in a rechargeable lightbulb and you're good to go. This is a nice option if you dream of fancy wall sconces framing a mirror or a piece of art but don't want the hassle of wiring them in.

In winter, I don't like coming back to a dark house, so I will turn on a smart lightbulb in a hallway lamp before I get home. If your hallway lacks light, pendant lights and lamps are a great way to brighten things up. Add mirrors strategically to reflect natural light and make the space feel brighter and more open.

Stamping your personality

The hallway is a great place to display your favourite trinkets and treasures. It's also a fun spot to show off your creative side. Create your own artwork or wall decor, like a DIY painting, a fabric wall hanging, or even framed fabric or wallpaper remnants. Add a gallery wall with a collection of your favourite photos, art or even mirrors. This adds a personal touch and makes the hallway more visually interesting. Head to page 44 for an idea for framing your memories.

Using a rug in your hallway will not only add to the aesthetic but also provide warmth and dampen down noise.

If space permits, bring the outside in with indoor or small potted plants; they can add freshness and a pop of colour.

Personalise your space by experimenting with different elements until you achieve a look that suits your taste and complements the rest of your home's design. For me, I just want my hallway to feel like a hug when I get home!

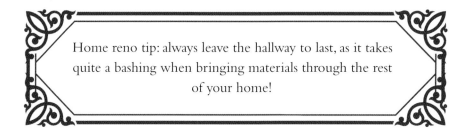

Home reno tip: always leave the hallway to last, as it takes quite a bashing when bringing materials through the rest of your home!

Hand Hotties

I love a sunrise walk, especially in spring when the mornings are getting brighter and the birds are singing away. To warm myself up, I pop a hand hottie in each pocket or inside my gloves (when I remember to bring them!). These little fellas are a big help in taking the sting out of the cold air, and they can be made with scrap fabric you have around the house.

I will give you two measurements, one for hands and one to use as a heating pad on shoulders and backs. As always, feel free to adjust these measurements to suit your needs.

What you need

Iron
Cotton or polycotton fabric
Tape measure and fabric marker
Fabric scissors
Sewing pins
Rice
Essential oil (optional)
Thread
Sewing machine (you can hand sew these too)

- Before cutting, iron the material to remove any wrinkles and get an even cut. Then, use a fabric marker to mark your measurements and cut out two pieces of material.

  ◊ For the hand warmers, cut two pieces of fabric 5 x 5 in (12½ x 12½ cm) and use a ½ in (1¼ cm) seam allowance.

  ◊ For the heated pad, cut a length of fabric 12 x 10 in (30 x 25 cm) and use a ½ in (1¼ cm) seam allowance.

- Let's make the hand hotties first. Place one piece of fabric on top of the other with the patterned (right) sides facing each other. Use safety pins to secure the pieces together.

- Leave an opening on one side so you can turn the pouch the right way out and fill it with rice. A gap of 1½ or 2 in (4 or 5 cm) should be fine, but if you have bigger hands, adjust the opening to suit.

- Straight stitch along all four sides of the pouch, remembering to leave this small gap on one side.

- Clip all four corners at a diagonal angle before turning the pouch the right way out, as this will

remove excess material and give you a neater, more pointed corner.

- If you want to add a scent, I recommend pouring your rice into a bowl, adding three to four drops of your preferred essential oil and mixing it with a spoon. I made the mistake of adding essential oil to the rice while it was inside the fabric pouch, and the oil slightly stained the material. Lavender oil is lovely for a soothing heat pad, but I also love citrus or orange oil for the hand warmers – their zingy scent is a nice wake-me-up in the mornings.

- You can use a spoon or fold some paper into a funnel to pour your rice into the pouch; fill it to about three-quarters.

- To close the pouch, you can either hand-sew the opening closed with a ladder stitch (see page 200) or fold the raw edges inwards and do a straight topstitch on your machine, on the side of the opening.

- For the larger heat pad, take your piece of material and fold it in half with the patterned sides facing each other. Follow the steps above and sew the three sides, leaving an opening large enough to fill with rice. Finally, close the opening with a hand stitch.

- To heat your hand hotties, I find 30–40 seconds in the microwave is plenty, but this will depend on the wattage. Start with 20 seconds and test as you go. For the larger heat pads, I heat for 1½ to 2 minutes.

- Before using your heat pad or hand hottie, gently touch it to your skin in case it feels too hot. They should stay warm for an hour or two.

- The larger heat pads can be used in place of a hot-water bottle and are great for soothing cramps or muscle pain. Both options make a lovely homemade gift, especially around Christmas!

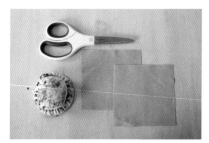
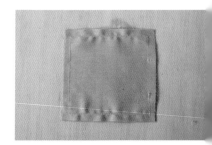

Lavender Wreath

While plants look and smell amazing in our gardens, we can extend their life inside the home by using them in crafts and home decor projects. I adore the scent of lavender, but the plant itself is not a fan of my soil and the wet Irish weather. Here are a few lessons I learned about growing lavender in my garden and instructions for a lovely lavender wreath.

Growing lavender

Lavender is a scented shrub, adored by bees, that comes in various varieties. The one I like to grow in my garden is an English lavender called hidcote. You can also get French and Spanish varieties; some are hardy or tender. I prefer English lavender because it is robust and will tolerate the Irish climate.

Plant your lavender in spring or autumn in well-drained soil and full sun. If you have a sunny and dry spot in the garden, your lavender will love it. Avoid shady and wet areas, as lavender won't be happy sitting in damp soil over winter. I prefer to grow it in pots, as I can move it easily and add some horticultural grit to the soil to get it right.

Once planted, prune your lavender around August or whenever it has finished flowering to prevent it from going leggy – in other words, when the base of the plant becomes woody. I am the queen of leggy lavender! Prune hard but avoid cutting into old wood. Instead, cut just above new growth on the stem.

When you harvest your lavender, wrap it in bunches, tie it with twine and let it dry. You can use lavender in many crafts. Below I share how to make a gorgeous lavender wreath, and on page 110, learn how to make lovely scented lavender pouches.

DIY lavender wreath

Creating wreaths is a fun way to use flowers from the garden, and they can be made with either dried or fresh flowers. Wreaths are big at Christmastime, but you can add one to a bare door to spruce it up whatever the season.

What you need

A wreath frame
Fresh or dried lavender stems
Floral wire
Wire cutters or scissors
Ribbon or twine

- For the wreath base, I am using a circular metal frame that I bought in a craft shop. You could also cut a base out of thick cardboard or use one made of straw. Pick up your florist wire in a craft shop, florist supply shop or online.

- I used fresh lavender for my wreath, which I bought from a shop in Wicklow that has harvest sales from mid-June to early August. If you only have a small supply, you can make a mini wreath or bulk it up with moss or other flowers. Or see if you can nab a bit more lavender from friends and neighbours!

- When picking lavender from the garden, cut the stems when the flowers are in full bloom.

- Trim the stems to a manageable length, removing any excess leaves or flowers from the lower part.

- Use floral wire to attach the stems to the frame, ensuring they overlap slightly. Twist the wire tails from each stem to secure the next one in place, repeating this process until the entire frame is covered. Try your best to distribute the flowers evenly.

- Once you've placed all the lavender, trim excess wire and stems that may be sticking out. Check for loose lavender stems and secure them with extra wire if needed. You can add a ribbon or any extra decorative elements before hanging it up.

- I find lavender wreaths quite delicate, so I prefer to hang them inside or in a sheltered spot outside, like a porch. If you use fresh lavender for your wreath, it will dry over time. You may notice some dried flowers falling onto the floor beneath; hang on to these and make lavender sachets for your bedroom (see page 110).

To store fresh lavender, keep it in a well-ventilated room and away from direct sunlight. I once tried to bring some fresh lavender home in my suitcase, but it didn't keep well due to lack of ventilation and developed mould.

Front Door Makeover

Your front door is like the handshake of the home. Pimping it with some new paint can be a quick and cost-effective way to upgrade the look and feel of your house and increase its curb appeal. It's also a great way to express your personality and play with colour.

On my travels, I love to stop and admire the different doorways: pastel-coloured ones in London, a hand-painted Moroccan door or a shabby Parisian one. They inspired me to spruce up my own bland white UPVC door.

When considering a door colour, think of the style of your home. Classic colours with a glossy finish can look elegant in a Victorian house with a solid wood door. If your home is more modern, darker tones of grey or black, or even teal, can give a contemporary look.

This is a project for late spring to early autumn, when the temperature is warmer and the days are longer, as once the temperature drops, the paint will take longer to cure and fully dry. Try to start first thing in the morning, to give yourself plenty of drying time!

What you need

Cloths
Sugar soap or degreaser
Fine grit sandpaper
Paint tray and roller
Primer and topcoat
Small paintbrush
Screwdriver to remove hardware (optional)

- Many paint brands are now selling 'paint your front door kits', which can be handy, so keep a lookout for these as they may be cheaper than buying your supplies individually.

- There are many primers on the market; choose the one designed for your surface, whether it is UPVC or wood. Using a primer helps the paint adhere to the surface, which will give you a long-lasting and more durable finish. Primer can also help seal porous surfaces, reducing the amount of topcoat needed and preventing stains from bleeding.

- Whether you choose a gloss, satin or eggshell finish, try picking a topcoat with a built-in UV filter to prevent fading.

- Begin by removing dirt and grime from the door, then use a degreaser or sugar soap to clean the surface.
- Next, use fine-grit sandpaper to lightly scuff (key) the surface. Fine-grit paper wrapped around a sanding block is perfect. Wipe away any dust from the sanding.
- Using a roller, apply one or two coats of primer. Check the tin for drying and re-coat times.
- Once your primer has thoroughly dried, apply two coats of your chosen topcoat with a roller, allowing drying time in between. I used a small paintbrush for the hard-to-reach areas.
- Handles, letterboxes and door knockers can be easily swapped and changed. I got this bee knocker to add some bling to my door. You can also add your house number using vinyl.
- While I was re-upping my front door, I decided to tile my plain front step too. Check out the tiled table project on page 194, as I followed the same steps here.

Stairs, Three Ways

Over the years, my stairs have had many makeovers. I took up the old brown carpet that was here when I moved in, painted a runner, and I even did a DIY carpet job by myself. You can really show your personality and style in this area of the house. I have kept my stairs neutral over the years, but I love seeing pretty ombre-painted stairs online and ones covered in thick, luscious carpet.

So often, when decorating our homes, this is the last space we think about — and most of the budget is spent by the time we reach the hallway. Let me share with you three ways I have styled my stairs without spending a fortune.

Removing old carpet

Let's begin by removing the old carpet. It's a lot easier and faster than you'd think, and it's a great way to save money when installing a new floor or stair carpet.

What you need

Dust mask, safety goggles, gloves
Knee pads (optional)
A sharp utility knife
Pry bar
Upholstery staple remover (optional)
Pliers
Flat head screwdriver
Hoover, rags, sugar soap, and bags for the clean up

- Old carpets can be dusty, so it's best to wear a dust mask, safety glasses and gloves for this project. Also, as there are a lot of staples, you should wear knee pads or take extra care to avoid kneeling on any nails or tack strips. I prefer to work from the top stair down, as it's less messy and easier on your body.
- Begin at the top of the stairs, moving any furniture that's in the way. Remove any carpet door strips and lift the carpet. When you lift it, you will probably find thin foam fabric; this is underlay. You can easily lift this with your hands and then remove any nails or tacks holding it in place.
- Use the pry bar to pry the tack strips away from the stairs. Tack strips are thin strips of wood with tiny nails studded into the wood that hold the carpet in place.

- You can use an upholstery staple remover or a flathead screwdriver and pliers to remove staples from the stairs. Use the flathead screwdriver to lift the staple, wiggle it out, and pull it with the pliers.
- When you reach the bottom of the stairs, it's time for the clean-up (and maybe a tea break!). I like to sweep up the tacks before hoovering, and then I'll use sugar soap and rags to wipe down the surface as I check for any staples I may have missed.
- Deciding what to do next is the fun part: you can sand, paint, stain or recarpet your new stairs.

Painting a stair runner

This is an easy way to transform the look of your stairs on a budget. If you plan to install a carpeted runner, you can follow these steps to paint your stairs before the carpet goes on.

When deciding what option is best for you, think of how much traffic your stairs get. Painted stairs are noisier than carpet, so if you have a busy home with many feet dancing up and down, this option might not be for you. I live in a dormer bungalow, so it's perfect for me. I don't have too much footfall, and my cat treated the old carpeted staircase as a giant scratcher! Painted stairs are also a fun choice for attic stairs and small staircases.

Another option is to paint the risers and leave the tread natural wood. Or, instead of paint, you could re-stain your stairs in a darker wood tone to suit your decor style.

What you need
———————

Sugar soap or degreaser and cloths
Fine grit sandpaper
Measuring tape and pencil
Painter's tape
Roller, paintbrush and tray
Primer
Topcoat

- When picking a topcoat, choose one that is not high gloss, as this can make the surface slippery. Some brands offer specific floor paints that are non-slip and durable. You can also mix an anti-slip additive with your regular paint – some companies will even add it to your paint when you go to get it mixed.
- Like with all good painting projects, begin by cleaning the surface of the wood with sugar soap or a degreaser, as this will remove any dirt the eye cannot see and leave you with a spotless surface.

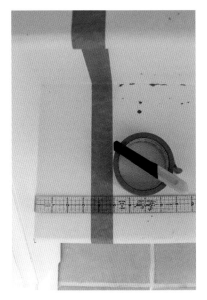

- Next, lightly sand the surface to key the wood. Wipe away (or hoover) any debris.

- Measure out the distance of your central runner. As a guide, I measured 5 in (12½ cm) from the side of the stairs on both sides inwards, which meant I had 5 in (12½ cm) on either side of the stair runner that I would paint white. An average width for a stair runner is around 27–28 in (68–71 cm), but if, like me, you have some funny-shaped stairs, you can adjust accordingly.

- Painter's tape is an excellent guide when painting the runner. After measuring and marking, lay the painter's tape along the lines, pressing it down as you go.

- I prefer to paint the sides first as they can be fiddly. Using a roller, apply primer and then two coats of topcoat, allowing each coat to dry before applying the next. A brush is handy for hard-to-reach areas.

- With the topcoat on the sides of the stairs, you can remove the painter's tape before painting your runner. When removing painter's tape, I like to wait for the paint to be touch dry, as removing it when wet can be messy and wet tape can touch off your floors and other areas.

- Now it's time to paint the runner. When the sides are fully dry, tape along their inner edge. The runner will be easier to paint as you can mainly use a roller. Follow the steps above and apply a coat of primer followed by two coats of topcoat. Allow the paint to dry, then remove the painter's tape.

- If you want, you can buy an extra anti-slip clear coat that you apply after the paint has dried.

Carpet runner

After my cat had scratched her way through my old carpet, I decided to have a go at recarpeting the stairs myself. Knowing that it might have the same fate as the last one, I didn't want to spend a huge amount of money, so I experimented by using mats from IKEA. You can buy lovely stair runners online or order a custom-sized one from a carpet shop, but if my rug hack suits your space and your style, it will save you a few steps (pardon pun!).

What you need

Measuring tape
Utility knife
Sharp scissors suitable for cutting fabric
Carpet underlay
Staple gun and staples
Runner or mats
Tack strips
Carpet trim or stair edging

- The mats I used on my stairs measured 65 x 105 cm (around 26 x 41 in), and I used six mats in total. If you are ordering a custom-sized runner, measure the stairs' width and length, including the height of the risers. Make sure to add some excess to allow for any mistakes.

- Since I was replacing an old carpet, I was able to reuse the underlay and tack strips that were in place. I checked them for damage and gave them a hoover to remove dust before reusing them. If you are placing new underlay, use a utility knife or sharp scissors to cut it to size. Then, use a staple gun to fix it to the stair tread and riser. (You can rent an electric staple gun suitable for stairs from most tool-hire companies.) Finally, attach the thin wooden tack strips to the back of the tread with nails.

- Now it is time to place your stair runner. Begin at the top of the stairs and work your way down, carefully tucking the carpet runner onto each step, riser, and around the edges.

- Cut any excess carpet on the last step and finish edges with carpet trim or stair edging.

- As I had anticipated, my cat Blondie adored my budget rug makeover, and a year later I admitted defeat and painted a stair runner instead. No matter how many scratching posts I made her, the giant stair cat scratcher was always her favourite!

Make a Splash

Bathroom

Ah, the bathroom – a place of daily rituals and occasional escape from the world's chaos. It's where you wake yourself up and wind yourself down, and sometimes, it's where you go for a few minutes of peace during a busy day.

For many of us, the bathroom can be a source of frustration. Small spaces, outdated designs (maybe a 1980s green sink set?) and lack of functionality can leave us less than inspired.

Like kitchens, bathrooms are another high-traffic area that can be expensive to transform.

But fear not: I have some tips and projects to help turn your bathroom into a personal oasis, a mini spa retreat. So, whether you are ready to reno or just want to revamp on a budget, this next chapter is for you.

Bathroom Revamp

As with kitchens, bathrooms are very expensive to renovate. In Ireland, a full bathroom reno can cost anywhere between €3,000 and €10,000 – or upwards, depending on the size of the room. Over the years, I have found smaller ways to refresh my bathroom space while I saved up to do major renovation work.

Before you begin your bathroom journey, it is always a good idea to spend time planning out your project, whether you're doing some DIY or bringing in contractors. Many people skip the planning stage, but it can prevent you from making costly mistakes.

Bathroom inspo

The first step in your revamp is to find inspiration, especially if you're still figuring out your style. Pinterest and Instagram are great starting points. You can search for similar-sized bathrooms to yours to see how people have best used their space. I like to create a dedicated Pinterest board for each project I do, then I add subsections (e.g. fittings, colour schemes, flooring) to my board and upload images directly.

To find your style, spend time scrolling and pin the images that please you the most! Review the ideas you have saved to find a common theme. Have you picked pictures with a distinctive colour palette or a particular tile pattern? Modern or vintage?

Making a mood board

When you have a rough idea of what you want, you can pull it together and create a mood board. If you decide to bring in an interior designer, builder or decorator, this will give them a clearer understanding of your style. If you're doing a DIY project, it can also keep you on track.

Mood boards are a great way to stay focused and avoid feeling overwhelmed by the endless images available on social media. While getting inspired by others is important, remember to add your personal touch to your mood board and make it your own. You can create a digital mood board on your phone or laptop, or make a physical mood board with paint/tile/fabric samples.

Showroom v sourcing it yourself

So now you have your mood board, you know what you want … what next?

You could visit some bathroom showrooms, get quotes, and see if they can execute your design choices. You could have a design consultation, pick what you want, and they arrange the contractors for you. The pro of going down this route is that you have the project arranged and organised for you; the con is that it could be expensive.

Another option is to buy the bathroom items yourself and arrange the contractors (or see what jobs you can do). Organising your own project may take longer, but it will be cheaper. And you can keep an eye out for sales on the items you want and source second-hand or salvaged items too.

To DIY or not to DIY

I love a good DIY – doing things yourself is a great way to save pennies. However, you should only undertake these jobs if you have the skills, as it might cost you more to repair if things go wrong.

Plumbing can be tricky for beginners. I once tried changing my bathroom tap, and it took me three times as long as it would have taken a pro. I spent most of that time figuring out how to turn off the water! In the end, I was happy I did it, but I won't be in a hurry to tackle any more plumbing jobs myself.

Maybe you are confident in one area, like tiling. By tackling that job yourself, you can spend on a contractor for the other areas of your project.

Here are some budget DIYs that you can do to refresh a bathroom space:

- **Mouldy sealant:** Over time, the sealant around the bath and shower can become discoloured and even mouldy. Before refreshing the sealant, all the old sealant must be removed and the area cleaned. Then, a bead of new sealant can be applied. A project like this is small but can make a massive difference to how clean your bathroom looks.

- **Regrout:** The grout between the tiles can also become discoloured and mouldy. Just like replacing sealant, remove the old grout before regrouting the area.

- **Replace bath panels:** Bath panels can become damaged or worn over time. Replacing them can give your bathroom a fresh look and make it more functional. I removed my old bath panel and used it as a template to measure my new one. If your old panel is in good shape, why not add some wood trim? You can follow the steps for Wainscoting on page 60.

- **Tiling:** Whether you want to replace old tiles or install new ones, tiling can give your bathroom a new lease of life. With a wide range of tiles available, you can choose the colour, pattern and style that best suits your taste. Practise some of the smaller tiling projects in this book to build your confidence.

- **Paint your tiles:** To refresh the look of your bathroom tiles without replacing them, consider painting them. With the proper prep and primer, you can achieve a professional finish. Personally, I'm not fond of the feel of painted tiles, but it is a great way to enhance what you have while you save some pennies to replace them.

- **Replace taps and fittings:** Old or leaking taps and fittings can be unsightly and lead to water damage. Replacing them with new, functional ones can improve the look and functionality of your bathroom.

- **Add shelves and storage:** Adding shelves and cabinets can help keep your bathroom organised and clutter-free. You can choose from various styles and materials to complement your decor. I managed to rescue an old bathroom cabinet that perfectly fit my space. Keep an eye on second-hand sites for some salvaged treasure.

- **Paint:** If you want to change the look of your bathroom without spending too much money, consider painting the walls or cabinets. Choose a colour that complements the existing fixtures and fittings in your bathroom.

- **Accessories:** Changing out your bathroom accessories, such as shower curtains, bathmats and towels, can make a big difference to the overall look of your bathroom. Choose items that match your style and colour scheme.

Chunky Towel Scrunchie

The scrunchie is back for book two, but this isn't any ordinary scrunchie: this is scrunchie 2.0. My friend Karen is a beauty guru, writer and photographer, and when she discovered these viral sensations, she asked me to make her some. Hands up, who gets soggy sleeves when washing their face? Well, these microfibre scrunchies will stop water dripping down your wrists while you're doing your morning and evening skincare routine. You can also use them to throw damp hair into a bun, as they will absorb excess moisture in your hair before you blow dry or style.

You can pick these scrunchies up for a few euro online, but if you have a packet of microfibre cloths and your sewing kit, have a go at making them yourself. If you'd rather not use microfibre for environmental reasons, cotton or old towels are both good alternatives, although these might not be quite as absorbent.

While I bring out my sewing machine here, this project is 100% hand-sew friendly, so follow the steps but do a straight hand stitch to sew instead of the machine.

What you need

Microfibre cloths (or cotton / an old towel)
Measuring tape
Fabric scissors
Fabric marker
Elastic
Thread
Sewing machine (or hand sewing needles)

- Microfibre cloths can be found in the kitchen or cleaning sections of most supermarkets, or in the pound shop. Keep an eye out for microfibre tea towels, as these are bigger and might be cheaper.
- For two scrunchies, I used two 12 x 12 in (30 x 30 cm) microfibre cloths and approximately 15 in (38 cm) of elastic (this will vary depending on the size of your wrist).
- I began by placing one towel on top of the other and doing a straight stitch down one side, so I ended up with one long piece of fabric, 12 x 23½ in (30 x 59 cm).
- I folded this cloth in half longways and cut down the long edge, leaving two pieces of fabric roughly 6 x 23½ in (15 x 59 cm), one for each scrunchie. The longer the length, the chunkier your scrunchie.

- Take your strip of fabric, fold it in half longways and straight stitch down the long edge, leaving both ends open (creating a tunnel). Then pull the material through so that it is the right way around and the seam is now inside the scrunchie.
- Grab some elastic, measure it against your wrist, and cut to size. Make sure it's not too tight on the wrist.
- Guide the elastic through the tunnel. This is the trickiest bit. Here's a tip: I added a safety pin to the front end of the elastic and wiggled my fingers in to grab the pin, then I pulled the elastic all the way through, removed the pin and tied a knot in the elastic.
- Now it's time to close the opening of your scrunchie. Fold over the raw edges and insert one folded end into the other to close the tunnel. Grab a pin to hold this in place. You have two options for closing: hand-sew it closed with a ladder stitch (see page 200) or straight stitch down the seam on the sewing machine. Hand sewing will give you a nicer finish, but if you have a batch of these to make, then finishing on the machine will be quicker.
- Time to test out your new towel scrunchies! I keep these near my sink and pop them on when I am doing my skincare, and they definitely stop those pesky drips of water from rolling down my arms. They're also very handy when washing dishes, to save your long sleeves getting soggy. They make great stocking fillers but would also be something easy to sew and sell at craft markets.

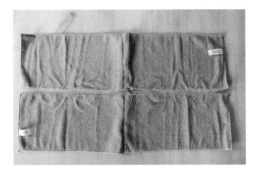
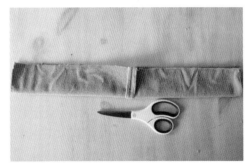

Heatless Hair Rollers

Finding ways to curl your hair without heat is an eternal mission for many women. With lots of tools on the market, it's hard to know which one to choose, so why not create your own and have that good hair day?

Sleeping with hair rollers in always makes me feel nostalgic. I remember my mam putting my hair in rags as a kid, and as a teen I would do a million plaits (hello, 1990s crimpy hair). The internet is full of hair-curling hacks, using everything from the belt of a dressing gown to empty loo rolls. The hair roller we make in this project is similar to the ones on sale in shops and online, but you can whip this up in under an hour using fabric you already have. This roller gives a voluminous blowout style and is suitable for all hair types.

What you need

Satin or silk material (or cotton)
Measuring tape, fabric marker and fabric scissors
Sewing clips or pins
Thread
Sewing machine
Fiberfill stuffing (or filler from a cushion)

- While you can use any fabric for this project, a satin or silk will help reduce frizz. But beware: these fabrics are more difficult to sew. Cotton is easier if you're just starting out on your sewing journey.
- Measure and mark 35 x 3½ in (90 x 9 cm) onto your fabric and cut with sharp fabric scissors. Use a ½-in (1¼ cm) seam allowance. If you have short hair and want a tight curl, make a narrower roller; for bigger, looser waves on long hair, make it wider.
- Fold the material in half, with the right sides facing each other lengthways, and clamp with a sewing clip. When working with silk or satin, I find clips better as pins can damage the material, but use whatever you have.
- Using your sewing machine, sew a straight line down the long edge (the one that is open and not folded) and stop before you reach the end. Then, with the needle still in the fabric, lift the presser foot and pivot the material so you are now stitching down the short edge. Stitch down the short edge and stop at the bottom, leaving the other short edge open.

- Turn the material the right way around. This can be tricky, so take your time.
- With the tunnel of fabric the right way out, take small chunks of fiberfill and stuff them into the opening. Push the filler down the length of the roller, packing it tightly.
- Once the roller is full, fold over the two raw edges of the opening and either hand stitch it closed with a ladder stitch (see page 200) or sew a straight line of topstitching down its length.

To use your hair roller

- Place the roller on top of your head and secure it at your hair parting with a claw clip.
- Beginning on one side, wrap the top sections of hair tightly around the roller – I prefer to wrap the hair away from my face – grabbing more hair as you go, until all your hair on one side is in the roller. Wrap the remaining hair around the length of the roller and secure it with a scrunchie. It might take a few goes to get your technique right, so make sure to practise before you try this for a night out.
- Follow the same steps on the other side.
- I find the roller works best on freshly washed hair that is almost dry. If the hair is too wet, it won't dry properly overnight. I sleep with my roller in, but if you find it uncomfortable, you can pop it in your hair for a few hours during the day. The longer the roller is in, the better the curl.
- When I remove the roller, I tease the curls with my brush and spritz them with hairspray to keep them in place. Using a heatless roller means my hair is less damaged, and it takes much less time than curling it with tongs or trying to blow dry it with round brushes. It's also great for travelling and holidays!

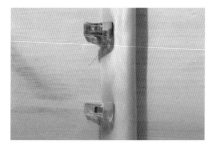

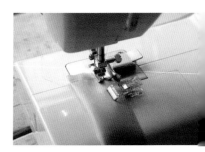

Makeup Headband

I love to wear a headband while doing my makeup and skincare, as it helps prevent any product from getting into my hairline (oh hey, greasy hair, you're not welcome here).

Dig into the fabric scrap basket for some decorative cotton to make your headband look pretty, and if you have any old towels, you can reuse them here. This is an excellent project for beginners and another one that can easily be hand sewn.

What you need

An old towel
Decorative cotton (optional)
Iron
Fabric scissors
Measuring tape
Fabric marker
Sewing pins
Sewing machine
Thread
Velcro

- If you'd like to create a batch of these – they're perfect as presents or to sell at a craft market – create a paper template that you can reuse. Iron your material before you begin.
- On your fabric (or paper template), measure and mark 25 x 2½ in (64 x 6½ cm) and curve each edge using the bottom of a glass or a small plate. Feel free to adjust the length – we all come in different shapes and sizes, so make sure your headband will be a comfortable fit.
- Cut two pieces of material, one in your decorative material and one towel piece. If you don't have any decorative material, use two pieces of towel instead.
- Place one piece of material on top of the other with the right sides facing each other and pin.
- Sew all around the fabric but leave a gap to turn it the right way out. I leave an opening of roughly 3 in (7½ cm), but I have small hands, so adjust accordingly. Use a ½-in (1¼ cm) seam allowance.
- Before turning the right way out, clip the curves of the curved edges and trim off any bulky towel material, taking care not to cut your seams.

- Turn the material right way out and press with your iron. Tuck in the raw edges of the opening and press them closed.
- Head back to your machine and do a topstitch all around your headband; this will close the opening and give it a decorative finish.

Velcro and alternatives

- Cut two strips of Velcro roughly 2 x ½ in (5 x 1¼ cm).
- You will add one piece of Velcro to the rounded edge of each end: one piece will go on the towel side, and the other will go on the opposite end of the patterned side.
- Add a dot of fabric glue onto the back of your Velcro, then place the Velcro on the material. Allow the glue to dry before using.
- Another option would be to use snap fasteners instead of Velcro and hand sew them on. Rummage through your sewing kit and see what you have before buying. Projects like these are great for using up what you already have in your sewing kit.

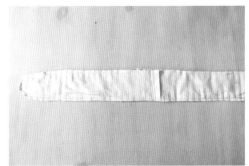

Simple Bath Stool

I adore those rustic stools and chairs you see in old French châteaus. If you come across one second-hand or in an antique shop, it can be pricey, so let's create one instead. Now, you might be thinking … I can't make a stool! But with this version, we are cheating a little by adding legs to a base and staining it to make it look aged.

It is a fantastic project for beginners to practise drilling in legs and working with a sander. It will boost your confidence, and you don't need a hammer and chisel. For me, this was also a recycling project. I made a DIY whiskey bar for my friends' wedding, so I thought it would be nice to reuse the wood from their big day, turn it into something practical but pretty for the home, and gift it back to them.

What you need

Wooden top
Stool legs
Degreaser
Old cloths or a sponge
Dust mask
Sandpaper (fine and medium grit)
Electric sander
Wood glue (optional)
Wire brush
Gloves
Wood stain
Clear varnish or wax
Pencil and measuring tape
Stool hardware
Drill
Screwdriver and screws

- You can buy furniture legs online in various heights and different styles. You'll see on page 105 that I created a second rustic stool and used hairpin legs on that one. Consider using the legs off an old table or stool from a second-hand site, as that might be cheaper, or you might even find something

for free in a skip! When choosing wood for the top, pick a nice thick piece, as it will be better at bearing weight.

- Give the top piece of wood a quick clean with some degreaser. Start with medium grit sandpaper to remove any old wax or varnish, then smooth with fine-grit sandpaper. Pop on a dust mask for the sandy parts of this project.

- I like to use an electric sander for the next part, as it is quicker and kinder to my wrists. Use the sander to smooth the corners of the wood and round them, to avoid your stool having any sharp edges. Check for any splits or damage and use wood glue to repair it if necessary.

- Sand all four legs of your stool. As my legs were round, I hand-sanded them with a block and sandpaper to remove the top layer of varnish. The wood of my legs was different from the wood of the base, so I wanted to get as much of the old varnish off as possible.

- Next, it's time to add some detail. Use a wire brush and brush in the direction of the wood grain. Wipe away any dust with a dry cloth before staining.

- Pop on your gloves and apply two or three layers of wood stain (see page 47 for more info) to the top piece. I went for a dark walnut shade, but you could also do a bleached whitewash or paint your stool.

- Next, apply the stain to the legs. My wood here was slightly different to the wood on top, but once I applied the stain all over, it started to look more uniform.

- When you are happy with the tone of the wood, it is time to seal. You can use a clear wax, clear

varnish or oil. I had a can of clear varnish in my stash, and I applied two coats. Sealing the wood will protect it and stop moisture damage, which is important if the stool is to be used in the bathroom.

- Once the varnish or wax has dried, grab your pencil and measuring tape to mark where you want to stick the legs. If you buy your legs, they will most likely come with the plate and hardware needed to attach them to a base. If not, you can find these parts in most hardware shops and online.

- I had to drill pilot holes into my wood base before adding the screws; depending on your base, you will likely have to do this too. Make sure not to drill the whole way through your wood base, and choose a screw the correct length so it doesn't pierce through the top of the wood. (This might sound obvious, but it's a mistake I've made in other projects!)

- Attach the leg hardware to the base and secure the screws with your screwdriver.

- Now, give your stool a quick test. Ensure the legs are steady with no wobbles and your stool is nice and sturdy.

- You could tweak this project and use longer legs to create a nightstand. A longer piece of wood could be used to make a bench or a mini one could be a plant stand. Take the idea and run with it!

Sweet Dreams

Bedroom

Your bedroom is the most personal and intimate space in your home. It's where you rest, reflect and recharge for the day ahead. However, sometimes our bedrooms can become cluttered and unwelcoming, making relaxation difficult. We've all been guilty of owning 'the chair' (myself included) – the place where we pile up clothes that are too dirty for the wardrobe but not dirty enough for the wash. We often neglect our bedrooms and invest more in decorating our living rooms and kitchens.

Your bedroom should reflect your personal style and preferences. Whether you want to create a peaceful oasis, a romantic retreat, or a vibrant space, it's entirely up to you. Your style here may differ from the other rooms in your home. I prefer a bright and neutral bedroom with some patterns that I can change throughout the seasons with textiles, but you might want a colourful space that energises you.

In this section, you will find some DIY projects that will help you create your perfect restful retreat. With a little bit of ingenuity and a touch of DIY magic, you can create a bedroom that welcomes you at the end of the day and inspires you as you start anew each morning.

Patterned Paint Roller

A fun way to add interest to a bare wall is to use a patterned paint roller. You'll find these artsy rollers in craft shops and online – you can even get vintage ones from the 1940s, so this idea of painted wallpaper has been around for a good while! They come in various designs, from wood grain to floral, and can be used on walls, furniture, fabric or even a floor. It gives a lovely hand-painted effect, and it is quicker to use, cheaper and less messy than wallpaper. So let's roll!

What you need

Patterned foam roller set
Paint tray
Scrap wood, cardboard or brown paper
Water-based wall paint
Rag

- Before painting, I did a bit of practice on a scrap piece of MDF. You could also use brown paper on a flat surface or a cardboard delivery box.
- Most patterned paint rollers come in three parts: there is an embossed roller and a foam roller, and these sit inside a frame with a handle.
- Insert the foam roller into the frame, and using a paint tray, roll it in water-based wall paint. Once you have enough paint on the foam roller, mount the patterned embossed roller into the frame. Keep a rag handy to clean away any excess paint.
- Do another practice roll to see if you're happy with the level of coverage, then begin in the corner of the room. Roll your first vertical pass down the edge of the wall, using the corner as your guide. As you roll, the surface of the patterned roller picks up a thin layer of paint from the foam roller. This first pass will serve as a guide for your second.
- After every third pass, remove the patterned roller and roll the foam roller in paint to reload.
- When I used this in a bedroom, I accidentally rolled a line upside down. I used a damp rag to wipe off the paint before it dried and then rolled a new pass correctly.
- Once you get the hang of the roller, no surface will be safe. Use it on brown paper to create patterned wrapping paper, or use fabric paint to create a pattern on plain material!

Lavender Pouches

Lavender is a natural moth deterrent, so these are perfect for wardrobes, drawers or anywhere you're storing clothes. I love to pop them in my suitcase when I travel for a fresh scent. You can make these sachets by hand or on your sewing machine – it's another great way to use up scraps. See page 76 for tips on growing lavender and instructions for a gorgeous lavender wreath.

What you need

Fabric
Iron
Sewing pins
Fabric scissors
Thread
Sewing machine or hand sewing needle
Lavender buds
Ribbon or string

- You can adjust the size of your pouches to suit their purpose or even get creative and try love hearts or circular shapes. For my sachets, I used some fabric I had left over from shortening a dress and cut two pieces of material, 4 x 6 in (10 x 15 cm). I like to iron my fabric before cutting to avoid any wonky cuts.
- Before joining the two pieces, hem one of the 4-in (10-cm) edges on each. Fold the raw edge over ⅕ in (½ cm), press with an iron, then press ⅕ in (½ cm) again, using pins to keep your hem in place. Topstitch a straight stitching line on this edge. The hemmed edge will be the top of the lavender bag.

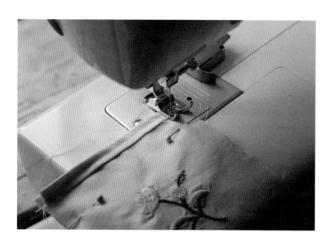

- Place one piece of fabric on top of the other with the patterned (right) sides facing each other. Line up the hems and pin them in place.

- Straight stitch the three sides, leaving the hemmed top open. I used a ⅕ in (½ cm) seam allowance, but you can use a ⅖ in (1 cm) allowance if your fabric frays easily.

- Once sewn, clip the corners diagonally to remove excess material and ensure a neater corner. Turn your pouch right side out.

- Use a teaspoon to fill your pouch with lavender buds until it is three-quarters full. Wrap some ribbon or a string around the top of the bag and secure it with a bow.

- You can now enjoy the delicious scent of lavender around the home. You can easily untie the pouches whenever you want to refresh the buds, and the old lavender can go in the compost.

Upcycled Bottle Lamp

Have you got a pretty bottle that you love the design of but don't know what to do with? Well, one option is to turn it into a stunning lamp, and it is now easier than ever – no electrical wiring skills involved!

A few years ago, I wanted to turn an old gin bottle into a lamp, but I was overwhelmed by the thought of drilling a hole into the bottle for a cable and fitting electrical hardware, as it was beyond my skill set. Nowadays, you can pick up a cheap bottle lamp kit, which sits into the neck of the bottle, quickly and easily transforming your bottle into a lamp.

It really is as easy as inserting a fitting and adding a lampshade and lightbulb. In this project, I'll run you through it and also share how I transformed one of my bottles with some DIY chalky paint.

What you need

Wall or acrylic paint
Baking soda
Glass bottle
Paintbrush
Sandpaper (optional)
Decorative tissue for découpage (optional)
PVA glue (or découpage glue)
Clear varnish
Bottle lamp kit
Lampshade

- I mixed up my DIY chalky paint first, then did a bit of découpage, before finally hooking up my bottle lamp. I am not a huge fan of chalk paint on furniture, but it is very cute on smaller projects like this and a great way to use up any old wall paint you might have in your stash.
- To create the textured matt paint, mix two parts paint to one part baking soda. Slowly add the baking soda to the paint and mix; if it gets too thick, add a teaspoon of water.
- Remove any labels from your bottle, then add two coats of your DIY paint mix and allow it to dry fully. Painting the second coat too soon can cause the first to lift off the glass. You can use light grit sandpaper to scuff areas on the bottle for a French shabby chic look.

- To decorate the bottle, you could hand paint some designs or do a little découpage. This is an artform that decorates objects with cut-out paper designs or fabric. This is what I did, and I used flowers from a paper napkin. I carefully cut out the floral images, then peeled off the napkin layers to leave just one ply. I applied clear PVA glue to the bottle – you can also buy specialist découpage glue. I laid the floral design on top of the glue and spread another layer of glue on top, sealing it to the bottle.
- Once you're happy with the design and the paints and glues have dried, give your bottle a coat of clear matt varnish (or gloss if you prefer a shine), as this will seal it and prevent chips or damage.
- Now all that is left is to add your lamp kit to the neck of your bottle and screw in your lampshade. Most lamp kits will have a rubber piece that you can squeeze into the bottleneck, kind of like a wine cork, and you can get them in various sizes depending on the width of the bottle's neck.

Want to make your lamp cordless? Use the same kit but remove the electrical cord (obviously when it's unplugged!). Add the fitting to the neck of the bottle, attach a lampshade, and then insert a USB rechargeable lightbulb – you can buy these online and in hardware stores. This is a great way to light up areas in your home where there's no power socket.

Meditation Mat

Yoga is my go-to for both relaxation and strength-building. I love a good deep stretch, and during the pandemic, I became a bit of an at-home YouTube yogi! Nowadays, I prefer an in-person class, but sometimes I will roll out my mat at home when I need a mindful moment. My favourite spot for this is my bedroom, as it gets lots of morning light, making it perfect for sun salutations.

During a class, I saw a fellow yogi with a fabric topper on her yoga mat. I loved the idea, so I decided to make one for myself. I recommend using your mat topper on top of your yoga mat for light poses, yin yoga, meditation and breathwork – it may not give you enough grip for more complex yoga poses and flows. You can also roll it up and use it as a bolster, place it under your knees or head when lying down, or sit on it as a support. You can even take it off the mat and get cosy under it for shavasana.

If you are not a fan of yoga, use this as a meditation mat instead, and fold it in half to create a small cushion.

What you need

Old blankets
Yoga mat
Measuring tape
Fabric scissors
Elastic
Sewing pins
Thread
Sewing machine
Iron

- Begin by laying your fabric out on the floor. Grab your yoga mat and use this as your template for making the topper.
- Place the mat on top of the fabric and cut the fabric slightly larger to allow for the seams. My yoga mat measured 72 x 24 in (182 x 60) cm. I cut a piece of material slightly wider and longer to allow for a ½-in (1¼ cm) seam allowance.
- For my topper, I'm using two old blankets: one is slightly chunky, the other light. (You'll see the chunky one again on page 190, where I make a garden cushion. One recycled blanket can do many projects!)

You could also use old bedsheets or any cotton or polycotton material you happen to have.

- Cut two pieces of fabric the same size.
- Lay one piece of material on the floor with the right (patterned) side facing you. Sandwich the other piece of material on top, with the right sides facing each other.
- Cut four strips of elastic 6 in (15 cm) in length. Pin the elastic to each corner (see image). These elastics will help your topper stay on your yoga mat.
- Pin the fabric around all four sides, leaving an opening on one side. The opening must be big enough to allow you to turn the material through the right way after sewing.
- Head to your machine and sew all four sides of the mat except for the opening. I used a ½ in (1¼ cm) seam allowance.
- Before turning the mat the right way out, trim any excess material and clip the corners at a diagonal.
- Iron your mat for a nice professional finish.
- Find the opening and stitch it closed. You have a few options for doing this. You can hand stitch the opening closed with a ladder stitch (see page 200); or fold in the opening and stitch it closed with a straight stitch on your sewing machine; or you can do a topstitch all around the mat. The final option will both close the opening and also give your mat a decorative finish.
- And now, it is time to stretch and relax. Lay the topper on your yoga mat and wrap the elastics around the corners. Whether you stretch, meditate or practise some deep breaths, I hope you feel refreshed and revived. Namaste.

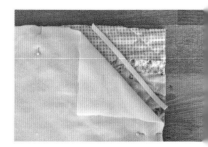
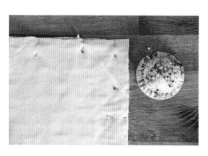
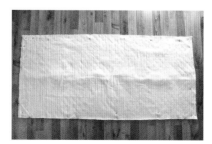

Board & Batten Panelling

When my nephew reached that age where he upgraded to a big boys' room, I had the honour of decorating his space. To add interest, I applied board-and-batten panelling to the walls and painted it his favourite colour, green. This is a lovely, calming colour, and it makes a change from blue in a boy's room.

Panelling is a nice way to add a pop of colour to a small room without making it feel tight, and if you feel like a change down the line, you can add wallpaper or vinyl above it. The actual application is easier than you'd think. You can customise it to fit any size of wall, and there are styles to suit everyone's taste, from this shaker style to wainscoting. As with other woodworking projects in the book, we'll use millimetres here for a precise cut.

What you need

MDF wood cut to size (or a kit)
Tape measure and pencil
Spirit level
Hand saw or electric circular saw
Adhesive suitable for wood and walls
Panel pins (nail) and hammer
Decorators caulk and gun
Cloths
Fine grit sandpaper
Primer and paint

- Some DIY stores sell panelling packs containing pre-cut MDF strips. While these are certainly a time saver, it can work out cheaper to buy a sheet of MDF and get it cut to your required size. Larger DIY stores sometimes offer a free wood-cutting service, so shop around. For this project, I used pre-cut MDF panels that were 1.2 meters long, 97 mm wide and 90 mm deep.

- Begin by figuring out what height you want your panelling to be. If you have an existing skirting board, measure from the top of the skirting board upwards and mark with a pencil. Next, measure the width of the wall and draw a line across using a spirit level. You can see in the photos that I used a laser level; these are super handy, so see if you can borrow one!

- Apply your horizontal panel strips to the pencil line you have drawn. If you need to trim any of the

wood strips, secure your wood to a table with clamps, measure and mark, then cut with either a hand saw or an electric circular saw.

- To secure the panel strips, apply a bead of adhesive to the back and place it on the wall, then hammer in some panel pins to keep it in place. Depending on your adhesive, you may not need panel pins, but they are handy to stop the wood from slipping as the adhesive dries. Before you start hammering, check for pipes or electrical wires to avoid piercing them.

- Now, let's work out how many panels you would like. I don't have a head for maths, so this was the trickiest part for me! I've included a little diagram here to help you visualise it:

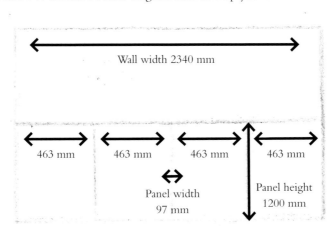

Measure the width of the wall minus the width of one panel strip. For example, one of my walls was 2340 mm long. The width of the wooden strip was 97 mm. **2340 – 97 = 2243**

I then divided this by four, since I was going to have four panels. **2243 ÷ 4 = 560**

The distance between panel strips will be 560 mm minus the width of one panel strip. **560 – 97 = 463**

So there should be a distance of **463 mm** between each strip. (Phew!)

- Before placing the panel strips on the wall, I leaned them against it and checked the measurements. You can mark the wall with your pencil and spirit level and check the distance is even between panels.

- Apply the vertical wood panel strips to the wall.

- Once all the panels are on the wall, it's time for the fun part: filling in gaps and joints with a decorators caulk. Pop a tube of caulk into a caulking gun, cut the applicator tip at a 45-degree angle, and apply a bead of caulk along the joints. Use a damp cloth over your finger to remove and smooth excess caulk.

- Use sandpaper to smooth joints and areas where you have filled holes from nails.

- Before painting, apply a primer suitable for MDF using a roller and paintbrush. Once all the primer has dried, apply two coats of your preferred topcoat in a colour of your choice.

Patchwork Cushion

While a patchwork cushion might sound intimidating to a beginner sewer, it is a perfect project for practising sewing straight lines and lining up seams. Also, it is a great way to use fabric scraps. I'm guilty of not being able to part with scraps – I have drawers full of them!

What you need

Cotton or polycotton fabric scraps
Ruler
Fabric scissors or a rotary cutter and cutting mat
Pins
Sewing machine
Thread
Iron
A 16-in (40-cm) cushion insert

- The cushion we're making here has an envelope back, which is perfect for beginners as you don't have to install a zip. It will have a patchwork piece on the front and two overlapping pieces of plain fabric – I've used one pink and one yellow – on the back. The overlapping back allows you to take the cushion insert in and out.

- To create the patchwork front piece, measure your scraps and use fabric scissors or a rotary cutter and mat to cut 16 squares, 4¾ x 4¾ in (12 x 12 cm). I used four squares each of four different cotton fabrics – have a rummage and see what you can find to mix and match.

- Take the fabric squares and lay them out in a pleasing pattern on a flat surface, then you're ready to start stitching.

- Begin by placing one fabric square on top of another with the patterned (right) sides of the material facing each other and pin.

- Using your sewing machine, sew a straight line of stitching along the right edge of the square using a seam allowance of ½ in (1¼ cm).

- You now have two squares attached. Next, lay the third square on top of the second square with the right sides facing each other and pin. Sew a straight line down the right edge like before.

- You now have three squares stitched together. Follow the steps above and add the fourth square.

- You now have a row of four squares stitched together. Put this aside and make another three rows in the same way.
- When you have all four rows made, open the seams and iron them flat, as this will give you a tidy, professional-looking seam.
- Now, let's stitch the rows together. Lay one row on top of another with the right sides of the fabric facing each other. Take time to line up the seams so they meet each other straight.
- Using a ½-in (1¼-cm) seam allowance, stitch the strips together down the long edge.
- Place the third strip onto the second strip with the right sides of the fabric facing each other and stitch together with a line of stitching down the long edge.
- Place the last strip onto the third strip with the right sides of the fabric facing each other and stitch the long edge like before.
- Iron all of the seams flat.
- To make the back panels, cut two pieces of plain fabric 16½ x 14 in (42 x 35½).
- To prevent the material from fraying at the opening, sew a hem onto one long edge of each. Using an iron, fold over ½ in (1¼ cm) and press, then fold over the same again and press. Secure the hem with some sewing pins while you sew a straight stitch down the hem.
- You will now sew all three panels together and form your cushion. The most important thing here is to make sure you face the right sides of your fabric together. Place the front patchwork panel on a flat surface with the patterned (right) side facing up. Lay a back panel of material on top, right side down, then add the third piece, right side down, and pin the fabric together.

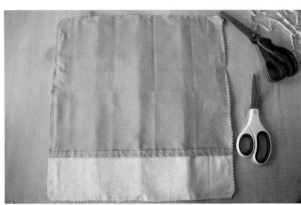

If you're feeling creative, you can also do patchwork
squares for the back panels.

- Take your cushion to the machine to sew. You are using a ½-in (1¼-cm) seam allowance. You can use the plate of your sewing machine as a guide. Make sure to start and end with a reverse stitch to stop your thread from unravelling. Next, sew around all sides.

- Before turning the fabric the right way out, you can zig-zag stitch the raw edge or use pinking shears to tidy up any raw material.

- To create a neat corner point, snip the corner of your cushion diagonally before turning it right side out.

- Open the back of the cushion and insert a cushion pad, as you would insert a pillow into a pillowcase. Give it a plump, and it's ready to go.

- And now it's time to admire your new patchwork cushion. You can place it on a couch, chair or bed to add a touch of colour and personality to your home.

Little Creatures

Kids & Pets

While putting together this book, Nicola, my amazing editor, and I had many mugs of tea sitting in the garden. We struggled to come up with a title for this section, and we felt guilty for putting pets and kids in the same chapter! But they do have many similarities. Both are adorable, unpredictable and chaotic at times, but they bring the most warmth and fun to our homes. (And they also live with us rent free!)

Over the years, I have shared my space with many paws. I felt the pain of losing them, but the joy I got from the time with them outweighed it all. I also have an energetic niece and nephew who love to transform my home when they come for sleepovers. Whether it's a tent in the living room or a colouring corner created, I see how differently they use my space. Our littles find adventure and fun everywhere and it's so refreshing to watch the world through their eyes.

What a family looks like has changed a lot over the years, and each family is unique. Some families live together under one roof, while others come to visit. Some of you might still be on the journey, dreaming of the day when littles come your way or when you're in your own pet-friendly home. Some of you have an 'urban family' of friends and neighbours. Whatever your situation, I hope this chapter will give you some ideas and inspiration for embracing the full spectrum of family life, encouraging you to think creatively and inclusively.

Children's Room Revamp

Hands up, who had walls full of boyband posters and a Groovy Chick bedspread from Argos? Kids' and teens' bedrooms have come a long way since our childhoods! While writing this book, I enjoyed helping my niece and nephew, Lily and Jack, transition into their 'big' rooms. I got to see the world through their eyes and quickly realised how different their decor needs were to mine.

I made sure to create an engaging play space in each of the rooms. While their clothes might be small, their toys are big, so I knew having enough storage was crucial. However, it wasn't just about functionality. I wanted this to be a fun, bespoke environment that reflected their unique personalities: a place where they could play, create, dream and rest.

Here are some of the things I learned from decorating their spaces.

Beds

You can think outside the box on this one! There are lots of alternatives these days to the classic single bed that takes up a lot of space.

For example, for my nephew, I got a half-bunk bed – also called a high sleeper or a loft or cabin bed – that can be reconfigured as he grows up. He is at an age where he wants space to play, so this raised bed gives him lots of floor space. It could also accommodate a desk or storage furniture in years to come.

For Lily's room, I got an extendable bed frame. There was an awkward stair bulkhead to work around, but in its shorter configuration, the frame fits perfectly into the nook. As she gets older, she can move the bed and extend it, but for now, she has what she needs: a cosy bed for her and extra floor space for her Barbies.

Just like toys, you can pick up lots of great second-hand children's furniture online. Most pieces are in good condition as people only use them for a few years, making them perfect for upcycling and reusing.

Colour

While my poor parents had to peel layers of BluTack and boyband posters off my walls, I am grateful to them for letting me reflect my personality and interests in my room as I was growing up.

Jack wanted his room to be green, but as it was small and low on natural light, I applied the green to the panelling (see page 119) and left the rest of the room white.

Now, my niece was more involved in the design process. She spent an hour walking through IKEA, thinking the display area was a giant dollhouse, which I totally get! She wanted wallpaper and loves pink, but we didn't want it to be too full-on, so I went for a neutral tone on the bottom and her wallpaper of choice on top.

Since interests change quickly, we stayed away from anything branded on the walls – keep the Disney and Barbie stuff in the play area!

Nowadays, you can get loads of self-adhesive wall decals and murals that are less messy and permanent than wallpaper. These are a renter-friendly option to add a splash of personality to the walls.

Storage

While we adults want more clothing storage, top priority here was toy storage and display. My nephew adores collecting plushies, so some plushie hammocks were a must.

Wall-mounted shelves, freestanding bookshelves and cube storage units with bins and baskets provide open storage space for books, toys and decorative items. You can also hang organisers on doors or walls to hold shoes, small toys or accessories, and benches or ottomans with hidden compartments make a lovely seating area as well as extra storage. Other ideas include over-the-door organisers, labelled bins and baskets, wall hooks for hanging items and rolling carts (perfect for art supplies).

Make sure that the storage is accessible. My niece can't reach up high and I don't want her climbing up to reach something, so using bins and baskets under her bed was a more thoughtful and safer way to store her toys.

Play areas

Even if space is tight, you can use a mat, play tent or beanbag to create a corner dedicated to play. As the kids grow up, you can add a desk to this corner for budding artists and creative hobbies.

My niece and nephew are fans of tech, so a reading nook was a must to help encourage some escapism through books and imagination instead. I used some old IKEA shelves from my home, cut them in half and secured them to the wall to create a tiny book nook for my niece.

Lighting

Both Jack and Lily wanted night lights for their rooms. I can relate to this, as I was scared of the dark as a kid. (Not going to lie – I still am, but nowadays I am more afraid of my electricity bill, so no night lights for me!)

LED lights are energy efficient, and you can even get smart bulbs that are controlled with your phone. Opt for soft, dimmable lighting that promotes a calm sleep environment.

Have fun with projector night lights, which project images or patterns onto the ceiling or a wall. You can get loads of different designs, but stars on a ceiling are my personal fave.

Safety

I had to consider things like outlet covers, corner guards and making sure furniture was extra sturdy and secure to withstand the rough and tumble of play. Take care when assembling any flat-pack furniture items, and check if pieces need to be anchored to a wall before use.

Overall, when revamping their bedrooms, my goal was to create a lasting space that wouldn't require frequent redecoration. A safe and relaxing environment where they could unwind and freely express their unique personalities. I am happy to report that Jack and Lily adored their new spaces, and I can't wait to see how their rooms evolve along with them!

Hot Air Balloon Lampshade

I absolutely love it when my niece Lily gives me a creative challenge! At first, I always feel a little overwhelmed, but then the excitement takes over. When she asked me to make her a hot air balloon lantern for her bedroom – inspired by ones we saw online – I set out to make her the most beautiful and unique hot air balloon lantern she had ever seen.

Not only are hot air balloons a hit when it comes to nursery decor and baby showers, but they can add a touch of whimsy to your tablescapes. Instead of a lamp, you could create free-standing hot air balloons in various sizes. Take the idea, make it your own and let your imagination soar.

What you need

Chinese lantern style lamp shade
Paint and brush
Jute rope
Scissors
Glue gun or craft glue
Mini basket (or make your own)
Patterned paper and twine (optional)
Scrap material and filler (optional)
Chopsticks or string

The lantern

- I used an IKEA Risbyn lamp for my project. Hang your lantern off something to make it easier to paint. For example, I used one of my camera tripod arms, but you could use a clothes hanger on a hook.

- I painted contrasting slices of colour on my lantern. To do this, I used the existing markings on the lantern as a guide. If your lantern has no marks, measure gaps evenly with a ruler and draw in the lines with a pencil.

- This project is perfect for using any old tester pots of paint, but you can use acrylic or chalk paint too. First, apply two coats of paint to the lantern. Most lanterns are made of paper, so be careful not to tear it while the paint it wet.

- Before moving on to the next stage, when the lantern is dry, test it on the light fitting with the light on, as you will be able to see any uneven areas of paint.

- To add detail, cut twine or thicker rope lengths and glue them along the lines you have painted. You can get creative with this and add as little or as much detail as you please. I used a glue gun here, which is quick, but I ended up with a few chunks of dried hot glue. If you have the time, a clear-drying craft glue would be better, but use what you have in your craft stash.

The basket

- Every hot air balloon needs a passenger basket! You can use an existing small basket, as I did – mine was an IKEA Lurpassa basket – or you can cut a milk carton or a cereal box and use the bottom. Paint it or wrap twine around it to create a basket effect.

- Whatever you're using, try to keep it as lightweight as possible, and allow for the weight of any mini passengers your little ones might want to put in.

The bunting (optional)

- Cut small triangles of patterned paper, apply a glue dot to the back of each and press onto a thin piece of string. While this sounds easy, working with small parts can be fiddly.

- Glue the bunting to the outside of the basket or swag a longer piece to the top of the hot air balloon.

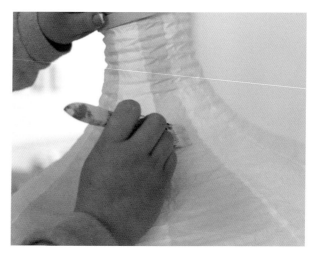

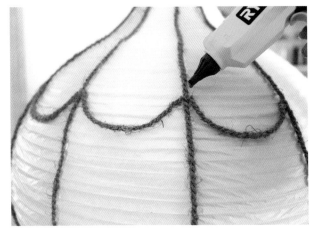
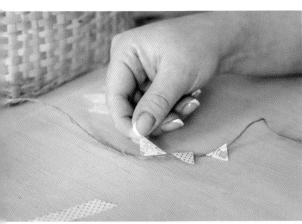

The sandbags (optional)

- Cut two pieces of fabric 1½ x 2 in (4 x 5 cm) and sandwich them together with the patterned (right) sides facing each other.
- Starting at the top corner of one of the long edges, straight stitch the three sides of the pouch, leaving an opening at the top.
- Clip the corners of the pouch and turn the right way out.
- Fill the pouch with some filler or scrap fabric and tie a piece of twine around the top to make it look like a mini sandbag.
- You can also hand stitch these mini sandbags or even make them with fabric glue.
- To attach the basket to the lantern, I used four chopsticks and glued them to the base and inside the basket. Another option is to use string to hang the basket from the lantern.

No Sew Book Pillow

A colouring cushion or book pillow is perfect for young readers and artists. It has built-in pockets for their favourite art supplies and books, and it doubles as extra back support when reading and colouring. The pillow can also lie across the lap to make reading and scribbling more comfortable.

These are perfect for travelling or can be used inside a play tent or reading nook. Like other projects in this book, feel free to customise this to suit your needs. I used a pillowcase here, but you can create a smaller version with an old cushion cover by following the steps below.

This is a perfect project for beginners – no sewing machine needed!

What you need

Pillowcase
Scrap fabric
Iron
Measuring tape, fabric marker and ruler
Scalloped or regular fabric scissors
Hemming tape

- We will be using hemming tape for this project. This is a special tape made of fine fleece that bonds fabrics together using the heat from an iron. It can be used on most fabrics and is washable. Most brands of hemming tape, such as Wonderweb/Wundaweb, come with instructions and will let you know of any material limitations.
- Gather your materials and iron your fabric. I find I make fewer mistakes when cutting my fabric if I iron the material before sewing (or, in this case, not sewing!).
- Lay your pillowcase flat on a table. Decide how many pockets you would like to have. For mine, I did one big pocket across the full width of the pillowcase (bunny fabric) and a smaller one at the front (pink and polkadots).
- I began with the large pocket. I added a piece of patterned cotton across the full width of the case, leaving a gap at the top. My pillow measured 18 x 29 in (46 x 74 cm), so I cut this first piece of material 13½ x 31 in (34 x 79 cm). The extra bit of width allowed me to fold over the raw edge of the fabric to create a hem.
- I used scalloped-edge scissors, also known as pinking shears, to cut my material. I find these help

prevent the raw edge of the material from fraying. But don't worry if you don't have them; just use sharp fabric scissors.

- Grab your first pocket piece and hemming tape. To create a hem on one of the long edges, fold over the raw edge by ⅖ in (1 cm, or the width of your hemming tape) and press a line into the fabric.

- You will apply the hemming tape to the non-patterned side of your material. Insert the hemming tape into that fold and press. Remove any excess hemming tape to protect your iron, as it will stick to it.

- Most hemming tapes need to be pressed for ten seconds. Make sure to do a pressing motion and not an ironing motion. Allow to set for ten minutes before testing the tape to see if it has fused. This hemmed piece will be the top of the pocket.

- Fold over the remaining raw edges on all three sides by ⅖ in (1 cm) and press.

- Now, you'll attach the first pocket piece to the front of the pillowcase. Place your pocket where you want it on the front of the pillowcase.

- Add the hemming tape between the pocket piece and the pillowcase on all three sides, close to the edges, and press.

- To turn this large pocket into two pockets, find the centre of the pocket, insert a strip of hemming tape vertically down the centre, and press. Doing this will create a fused line down the centre, giving you two pockets.

- After this, have fun adding more pockets by following the steps above. Not too many, though, as the weight of too many books can cause the material to pull. Fill with your favourite kids' books or art supplies, and you're ready to go!

Salvaged Table & Chairs

Nowadays, lots of cool kids' furniture is readily available and cheap to buy. But unfortunately, many pieces end up in the dump when they get damaged or are no longer needed. I stumbled across this bashed-up table and chair set that had been left outside in the rain. While most people would chuck it away, I saw the potential!

The original MDF bases were water damaged and warped. I decided to save the wood frames and use the old pieces as a template to create new bases for the chairs and table.

If you find a discarded piece of furniture that looks a bit scary, check the main frame first for any damage. Look for missing screws and bolts, split wood, mould, and other signs of wear. Most pieces look worse than they are and just need a good sugar soap scrub to bring them back to life. However, some might have more damage and could need parts to be replaced or repaired.

What you need

Salvaged table and chairs
Pencil
A sheet of MDF
Clamps
Jigsaw or hand saw
Sugar soap
Sandpaper
Paint and primer
Paint roller and tray
Stencil and brush
Clear varnish

Prep and paint

- I disassembled my table and chairs to remove the damaged MDF pieces. I laid those pieces onto a new sheet of MDF that was the same thickness as the old piece. Then, using a pencil, I traced the shape of the old parts onto the MDF. I had three in total, a piece for each chair and a new tabletop piece.
- I clamped my wood to a sturdy table and carefully cut out the new wood pieces with my jigsaw. You

could also use a hand saw for this, but factor in some extra time for cutting. Thinner MDF is easy to cut by hand.

- Next, I scrubbed the wooden frame to get it ready for paint. I also wanted to remove any grime and bacteria as it had been in the rain.

- I followed my usual steps for painting (see page 201 for more details). After a good prep of sugar soap and a light sanding, I applied one coat of primer followed by two coats of a satin finish paint, allowing each coat to dry fully in between.

Stencil and varnish

- Choose a stencil that you like and one that fits the furniture surface. You can trim it if it is too large or use sections of the stencil instead of the whole thing.

- Next, prepare the furniture thoroughly and create a smooth surface. Secure the stencil firmly with tape to avoid slipping or moving when applying paint. (Practice on a sample surface before using the stencil directly.)

- Use a foam or stencil brush to apply paint in a dabbing or swirling motion. Carefully remove the stencil to avoid smudging. I like to lift the stencil when the paint is still wet. If the paint has dried, the stencil is likely to stick to the surface, causing the paint to lift when removing it.

- After stencilling, I applied two coats of water-based clear varnish to seal the new table and chair tops. I wanted to protect them and make them wipeable.

Assembly

- Now it was time to re-assemble the pieces. I tightened each screw carefully and checked that the new MDF bases were slotting in perfectly to the old frames. I made sure to test the weight before giving this set to my niece and nephew.

The children were overjoyed with their new table and chairs set, but I got the most joy from reviving and rescuing it!

Play Kitchen Makeovers

Just as the kitchen is the heart of the home, the mini kitchen is the heart of the play corner. I love playing pretend kitchen with my niece and nephew and have consumed many imaginary meals over the years. These toys are great for stimulating a child's imagination, curiosity and creativity.

When purchased new, a play kitchen can cost anywhere from €80 up to €200, but you can pick one up for a fraction of the price (or free!) online or second-hand.

Perfectly pink

This kitchen makeover was for my bestie's nieces, and their only demand was that it be 'pink and girly'. I disassembled the kitchen to make things easier and gave it a pretty paint job (see page 201 for my painting guide).

This was back in 2018, when marble was all the rage, so I used some marble contact paper on the countertop. This is a self-adhesive vinyl that can be applied to most surfaces and it is wipeable, washable and easy to remove. It is also cheap, starting at around €5 a roll.

Here are some quick tips for applying contact paper:

- Clean the surface thoroughly.
- Measure and cut the contact paper accurately.
- Practise on a small area first.
- Start with a small section, smoothing out air bubbles as you go.
- Work in small areas, gradually peeling away the backing paper.
- Trim excess paper for a clean finish.
- Use heat to help adhere stubborn corners or edges.
- Remove and reposition if necessary.

Most importantly, take your time. And don't worry – contact paper is much better these days than it was years ago when we were making a sticky mess trying to cover our schoolbooks!

To finish up, I gave this kitchen some gold hardware using spray paint. My hardware was plastic, which would cause some spray paints to peel, so be sure to use a spray that's suitable for your surface and test a small area first.

Natural beauty

The next kitchen I rescued was a challenge because I had to do a lot of paint stripping. It had been spray painted with a pebble effect paint, meaning it had lots of grainy sand bits that were a nightmare to remove. At first I tried an eco-friendly paint stripper, but unfortunately, it wasn't strong enough. So I used my heat gun and a wallpaper scraper to lift off as much as possible before sanding. Happily, I found some beautiful wood underneath, so I kept stripping and sanding until the pebble spray paint was no more.

After sanding the wood, I did a half-paint/half-stained look. There was a good reason for this: the places that were the hardest to remove the old paint from had some damage, so I primed these areas and then applied two coats of satinwood paint.

To get a whitewashed effect on the wood, I used half white paint and half water. Using a sponge, I washed the mixture over the wood and wiped away any excess with a dry cloth. Doing this lightened the tone of the wood but still showed the grain underneath. Once I was happy with the level of whitewashing and it had dried, I sealed it with clear coats of water-based varnish.

I was so pleased with how this turned out. Now all my kitchen needed was a sprinkle of imagination and a dash of make-believe from some tiny chefs!

Perfectly pink (before)

Natural beauty (before)

Natural beauty (after)

Painted Playhouses

The garden is not only an escape for adults but also another space for little ones to explore. A garden playhouse can be a charming abode for epic tea parties or secret club meetings (no adults allowed!)

You can easily pick up an old playhouse second-hand, but a little tip: these items are more popular in the summer months, and the free ones get snapped up. So you've gotta be quick, or hang on and get one later in the season. Here are two playhouses that I had the pleasure of making over.

Plastic fantastic

The plastic playhouse has been around for years, and rightly so, as it is indestructible and can survive the elements. Over time its colour can fade from the sun's UV rays but fear not – you can revive it with a lick of paint.

When painting a plastic playhouse, follow my usual rules of prep, prime, paint (see page 201). Use an outdoor paint with a UV filter that is suitable for the surface, or you can use a special primer underneath designed to adhere to difficult surfaces.

These playhouses are super easy to disassemble, and most will have small plastic screws that are easy to open. Spiders love to use them as their home over winter – when painting this one, I had to serve an eviction notice to a few that were hiding underneath the roof. It's best to cover your playhouse in the colder months, not just to prevent unwanted guests but also to protect it from the elements.

If you have a paint sprayer, that would be handy, but you can also use a paint roller and brush. I painted the bricks, door and roof in shades of pink and went for a neutral base on the rest. I used my vinyl cutting machine to create a house number and added some details to the postbox, and I drilled in a bell on the side for fun.

Wood, also good!

When working with a wooden playhouse, you will have more colour options, as hardware stores are packed to the brim with outdoor paints and stains suitable for wood.

I followed my usual steps regarding the paint job (see page 201) and then had fun with the

accessories! I added mini curtains, an extra shelf (so we could have a shop, of course) and a canopy. Just remember that when making modifications, you must ensure they are age appropriate and don't pose a safety risk, and let the owners know they should be regularly checked for any signs of deterioration or damage.

To create mini curtains for your project, follow the steps for the Easy Sew Curtain on page 25. You can modify by using Velcro to stick them to the window.

I used a flat-pack pine shelf and painted it, making sure it was secure and that it wasn't too heavy for the existing frame.

For the canopy, I got myself two triangular hanging basket hooks and secured them to the wood with appropriate screws. I then stitched a piece of fabric and used Velcro to stick this to the frame of the canopy.

One of the best feelings in the world is when I finish a project like this and get to hand it over, seeing the pure joy on the kids' faces as they play with it. It brings me immense happiness to know that I've created something that gives them so much fun and a space in the garden that's just for them.

Wood before (above) and after (left)

Plastic before (top) and after (above)

Pawfect Scratching Post

If you are a cat owner, you'll be all too familiar with the sound of your feline friend picking at your couches. Scratching posts can be costly, especially the bigger ones, so let's create a budget-friendly, eco-friendly one of our own!

When rummaging through the recycle bin, pick out sturdy items – cylinders and tubes work especially well. I used an old porridge drum and a cardboard snack tube. You can also use tin cans or even scrap wood. This project really is as easy as wrapping twine and gluing.

What you need

Clean, sturdy items from the recycle bin
Jute rope
Glue gun and glue sticks
Cardboard
Scissors

- I used hot glue sticks from the DIY store, as these are usually stronger than those from a craft shop. My creation was made by covering a large cylinder, a smaller tube and a circular piece of cardboard with jute and then gluing them all together. Yours might look different, based on the items you're recycling.
- Begin by applying a bead of glue onto the lower end of your item, then wrap the jute cord around. Wrap the cord tightly, applying more glue as you move upwards. When you get to the top, carefully glue the end and tuck it into the last piece of cord to stop it unravelling.

- I sat my cylinder and tube on a circular base, but you can tweak this and use a different shape if you like. You could use wood instead of cardboard, or another flattish recycled item.
- I used a plate as a template and traced a circle onto cardboard, then I cut it out carefully.
- Starting in the centre, I applied a bead of glue and glued down my jute cord. I kept rolling the cord around the cardboard base, working from the centre outwards and gluing as I went.
- Finally, I stuck the cylinder and tube onto the base by gluing the bottom and firmly pressing down.
- If your kitty isn't an instant fan, you can rub some catnip into the scratcher to entice them, or place treats around it.
- Scratching is a natural behaviour for furry friends. They do it to mark their territory, stretch their muscles and sharpen their claws. Place a few of these scratching posts around the home – I keep some near the sofa. Whenever those little paws try to attack the couch, I redirect them and praise them when they use these recycled scratching posts instead!

Recycled Pet Bed

Pets like to find their own comfortable spots to rest in your home. Dogs might try to sneak onto the bed or snuggle on the couch, while cats can turn a cardboard box into a cosy napping place.

You can never have too many pet beds or cushions around the house. And they're portable, so you can bring them along when away from home or travelling to the vet as a source of comfort for your furry friend.

I am using an old, thin rug to create this simple bed. Thinner fabrics like satin, light cotton and velvet can show up claw marks, so this old rug is perfect because marks are less visible.

What you need

Old material (or new, if you are feeling fancy!)
Sewing pins
Sewing machine
Thread
Fabric scissors
Old pillow or filling
Hand sewing needle

• Ideally, you want to be able to pop your pet bed in the washing machine to freshen it up. So when picking your material, check the washing instructions on the care label and jot them down somewhere. Old bedsheets, blankets, light rugs and even tent materials work really well. Most thicker materials can be spot-cleaned often and occasionally popped into the washing machine for a full freshen-up.

- Begin by deciding how big or small you would like your pet bed. My rug measured 23½ x 35 in (60 x 90 cm), and I folded the material in half to create my bed.

- Fold the material with the patterned (right) sides facing each other and pin. If using a thicker material, swap the needle in your machine for a thicker one and adjust the tension setting. For thick materials like denim and leather, a tension of 3.5 to 4.5 is recommended, but test first on some scrap material.

- Straight stitch two sides – a short edge and a long edge – leaving the second short edge open.

- Trim off any excess bulky material and cut the corners diagonally. Turn the material right way out and gently push out the corners.

- I used the filler from a cushion here. I wanted it to have a bit of squish, so I didn't pack it too tight.

- Fold over the opened edges and pin them into place so no raw edge is exposed. I used a hand-sewing needle and thread and did a ladder stitch (see page 200) to close the opening.

- You can tweak this design by adding a zipper or Velcro and inserting a pillow instead. I wanted to keep this bed simple and beginner-friendly, but if you are more advanced, these options would make washing and drying easier.

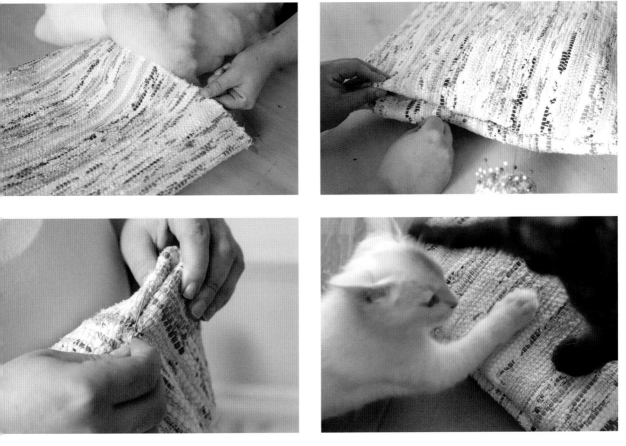

Cute Cat Collar

If your cat's collar is looking tired, why not repurpose the old parts and make a new one? It's a great way to use up leftover fabric scraps, and you can have fun incorporating colours and patterns to highlight their unique personality.

When making a collar for a cat, it is important to use safety clasps to stop them getting tangled or caught while exploring. The safety clasps will detach, allowing them to escape unharmed. Most collars nowadays have them, but do double-check, especially if you're using parts from an old collar.

Lightweight cotton material is perfect for this project. You can wash cotton collars in the machine, and the fabric is less likely to irritate. I used some leftover material I had from clothes alterations.

What you need

Fabric
Measuring tape
Fabric marker and fabric scissors
Iron
Sewing pins
Thread
Sewing machine
Old collar

- You can use an old cat collar as a template, but if you don't have one, here are the measurements I used: For a kitten collar, cut one strip of material to 12 x 1¼ in (30 x 3 cm); for a cat collar, cut one strip of material to 15 x 2⅓ in (38 x 6 cm).
- Mark your measurements onto your material with a marker and ruler and cut, then fold it in half lengthwise and press with an iron. If using a patterned fabric, fold the material with the non-patterned (wrong) sides facing each other.
- Open the material back out flat, and you will now have a line down the centre to use as a guide.
- Next, fold in the two long sides towards the centre line and press.
- You will now have the two raw edges of the material facing the centre. Fold the fabric in half, tucking in the raw edges and press; you can use some sewing pins to secure the material.
- Head to the sewing machine and do a straight line of topstitching down each side of the fabric strap.

Since the kitten collar (the white one in the photos) is very narrow, one line of stitching is perfect.

- On each end of the strap, fold over the raw material once and once again and iron to create a hem. Don't worry about sewing this hem; we will do that later.

- Now, it's time to bring in the old collar hardware. On one end of the strap, thread through the hardware piece with a bar in the centre. With this piece of hardware at the end of the strap, fold over the raw edge of the material and sew a straight line of stitching across.

- Thread one clasp through the other end of the strap and leave it in its centre.

- Thread the unsewn other end of the strap through the bar hardware. Add the last remaining clasp to the end of the material you have threaded through. Fold over the raw edges and sew a straight line of stitching to sew this clasp in place. You have now created your collar.

- When fitting your pet's collar, adjust the size and make sure you can fit a finger between the collar and neck. Young animals grow quickly over a short period, so check the fitting of their collars frequently. It is recommended that you microchip your pet in addition to using a collar, as this will make it easier for someone to contact you if they are found.

> To create a collar for a dog, follow the same steps but use clasps and fittings suitable for dogs instead. They don't require safety clips like the ones on a cat collar.

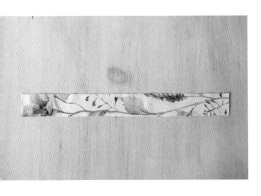
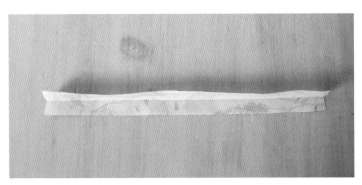
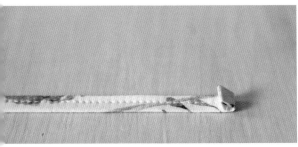
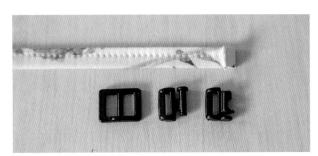

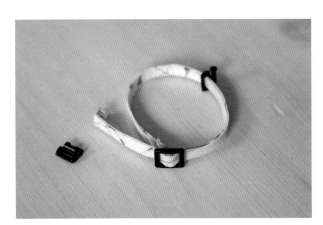

Nature & Nurture

Garden

Over the years, the garden has become my favourite room in my home. When I was younger, I saw gardening as a chore. Cutting the grass was a task, fallen leaves were a burden. But over time, the garden became a hive of activity for me and the wildlife with whom I share it. Those fallen leaves are now used as mulch and make valuable leaf mould for my soil. My weekly stroll with the lawnmower is an escape from reality as I load up on my vitamin G.

Mother Nature teaches me many lessons, from patience to abundance, learning from setbacks and adapting to the conditions she throws at me.

While gardens are pretty to look at, add value to your home and create a space to entertain, they are also healing. Come springtime, when the mornings are a little brighter, nothing gives me more joy than an early potter around the garden with my mug of tea, listening to the morning chorus of chirping birds and seeing what is growing. Anytime I feel overwhelmed, anxious or low, I head to my garden to get lost in it. An hour or two of escapism and I feel satisfied and grounded.

A lot of unseen magic happens in the garden. Worms munch away under the soil, bees are busy buzzing around, and if you're lucky like me, you might have a spiky friend who makes a messy corner their home. I never feel like I own my garden, but I see myself as the caretaker, carefully creating a space for nature to thrive.

Gardening can also open up a new community. Many of my plants are grown from cuttings, dividings or seeds from my neighbours' gardens. I have pals who I chat with because of a mutual love of each other's plants and green spaces.

If you don't have a garden, don't worry, as you can get the same joy from growing in containers and pots, or you can create a green space on a balcony or wall.

In this section, I hope you are inspired to flex your green thumb and do some garden projects with me. All you need is patience, persistence, and a willingness to try and fail and learn.

Growing Your Garden

I gardened backwards over the years. When I began, I didn't know what soil type I had (or even that there were different soil types!) so I popped plants in the ground where I liked them, not necessarily where they would thrive. I certainly didn't know my annuals from my perennials.

I made many mistakes in my garden, which were my biggest lessons. Some plants forgave me, while others perished and ended up in the compost.

As in other areas of the home, landscaping and creating your dream garden can be costly. However, you can do it on a smaller budget too; all you need is a willingness to get into the mud and patience to grow.

While giving a room a makeover can provide instant results, creating a garden can take longer, but it is just as rewarding. Plants will develop and thrive year after year, and you can edit out or layer onto your garden as you wish. Let me share my tips for getting your garden started.

Observe and study

When planning your garden, take time to get to know it properly. Observe where the sun is at different times of the day; identify shaded areas and sunny areas. A bad habit of mine was planting sun-loving plants in the shade and vice versa.

Healthy soil means healthy plants. Head out to your garden, take a handful of earth and add some water until it becomes pliable. Roll it into a ball and observe how much sand, silt and clay is in the soil, as this will help you understand the level of drainage. If the soil crumbles when you roll it into a ball, then it is on the sandier side. If the soil holds together well or feels much finer than sand, it is more on the clay side. Sandy soils feel like granulated sugar or salt when rubbed together, and clay soils feel sticky when moist, like plasticine.

I learned that I have heavy clay soil in some areas of my garden. Heavy clay soil can become compacted easily, so it's hard for plant roots to penetrate and for water to drain. During dry weather, clay soil can become hard and cracked, and during wet weather, it can become muddy and heavy.

But don't worry if you have heavy clay soil, as you can improve its quality by adding well-rotted organic matter. For example, mixing compost, bark or aged farmyard manure into the soil will improve the structure, making it easier to work with, and it will also improve drainage.

I mulched my flowerbeds in springtime for the past few years and noticed a massive improvement

in my soil and plants. I order a large bag of fine bark mulch in early spring and spread an even layer over the soil. Mulch has many benefits. It helps to retain moisture and cut down on the number of weeds. It also improves the soil by adding organic matter as it decomposes.

If you have space in your garden, you can create your own compost. Or, like me, you can nick some from your fellow gardeners. During signings for my first book, Brenda, one of the sales team at my publishing house, used to give me bags of her finest well-rotted horse and farmyard manure for my garden. We'd be in the car park with our boots open, swapping garden mulch. Her home-made compost was magic to my roses, and they thrived on it.

The ideal soil pH is around 6.5. A pH in the range of 5.5 to 7.5 allows a wide range of plants to thrive, as nutrients are at their highest and there's plenty of bacterial and earthworm activity. But some plants, like rhododendrons and camellias, prefer more acidic soils. When you are planning your planting, do some research on the type of soil your new plant likes and then purchase a soil-testing kit from a garden centre or online to see what you're dealing with. In the long run, this will save you heartache, unlike me, who learned the hard way!

The big picture

Ask yourself what you want your garden to be. Is it for entertaining, relaxing or growing your own food? This is a great way to begin your journey.

If you want your garden for entertaining, plan a larger seating area with tables, garden sofas or a barbeque area. If you'd like it to be a place for relaxing, allow more room for flower beds and a smaller entertaining area. If you want to attract insects and wildlife, add a pond or a wildflower patch, or plant native shrubs and trees.

Just like with interiors, there are plenty of garden trends and styles to suit everyone, from cottage to modern. If you need help finding your gardening style, head out and visit parks and open houses. The show gardens at flower shows are great for inspiration too.

However, while you might admire a garden full to the brim with flowers in borders, you might not have the time to maintain it. So make sure to think, too, about how much of your life you can dedicate to your garden each week. The great thing about gardens is that you can layer them over time. Start with a simple and easy-to-maintain space now, and you can always add more in the future.

Do a doodle

Sketching ideas is a great way to keep yourself on track when designing your garden. It is also handy if you choose to get the pros in, as you can share your sketches with a garden designer or landscaper.

When sketching out your garden, take note of the shady/sunny areas, areas where the soil may need improvement, etc. Also, consider practical things like sheds, compost areas and a water butt. For example, I should have left space for a decent compost area in my garden, and it's much harder to add one in now.

With summers becoming drier and hotter, it is also handy to think of a water system. I recently got a small water butt to sit behind my greenhouse and collect rainwater for watering during the hot months. I am a watering can kind of gal, and while it can be a chore, I enjoy a summer evening in the garden watering and pottering among the flowers.

There are many irrigation systems that you can install; you can even get fancy smart systems that work off apps. To conserve water, I am trying to adapt and pick more drought-tolerant plants for the drier areas of the garden.

Hardscaping

Hardscaping means the non-living elements of your garden design such as pathways, patios, decks, walls and other structures. You can use materials like concrete, brick, stone or wood to create practical and attractive elements, and it's a good way to zone your garden: a seating area for that summer morning mug of tea, a dining area for entertaining, or a fire pit area for cosy evenings watching the sunset. Have fun creating pathways in your garden or use wood to build raised beds and a veggie patch.

Keep an eye on salvage yards and second-hand sites for reclaimed items, as you may save money and get something unique for your garden.

I roped my brothers in to help me do some hardscaping one winter. Renting power tools for a couple of days can cut the cost of creating your dream garden, and it's also fun. While my brothers probably cursed me at the time when shovelling wheelbarrows of stone, we did have a laugh that weekend!

Plant planning

The cheapest option when creating a garden is to grow plants from seed. It requires patience, but the payoff is worth it. You can also take cuttings from established plants and divide certain plants at the root.

One of my biggest lessons in the garden was to use more shrubs and evergreen plants. I adore flowering perennials, but I noticed I would have gaps throughout the year in the borders, so I added more evergreen plants and shrubs to create interest and fullness. I prefer to spend money on perennials and shrubs and grow annual flowering plants from seed in springtime.

One of my favourite celeb gardeners, Carol Klein, is the queen of cuttings. If you have established plants in your garden, check out her books and find her on YouTube for tips on taking cuttings from them.

Consider planting trees in your garden, which are great for attracting birds and providing shade or privacy. There are many varieties of tree suitable for smaller gardens too.

If planning your planting is overwhelming, you can search online for free planting plans or chat with a horticulturist or garden designer.

Maintenance

I spend roughly one afternoon a week in my garden. My weekly garden jobs include mowing (although I am trying to cut back), weeding and general tidying up. In springtime, I am busy sowing seeds and checking in on seedlings. Then, come summer, I am planting annuals and veggies and staking perennials up where needed. In autumn, I mulch with leaves, plant spring bulbs and divide plants, before joining the garden to rest in winter.

While I love to create and find jobs in the garden, I know that not everyone has the time. But even an hour here and there is enough to keep on top of it. Little and often is a great lesson I have learned.

Going Potty!

If you are short on space but still want a show garden, growing plants in containers is a fantastic option. You can grow many perennials and annuals in pots and even some veggies. It's a perfect way to create a garden on an apartment balcony or a concreted patio area, or to make a focal point within a larger space. If you have a balcony, for example, and want to hide a view, you could grow some bamboo in a container to draw the eye away. Some small trees can also be grown in containers – in my garden, I have an olive tree and a small coronet apple tree growing happily in their pots.

You can use containers to fill gaps in your garden too. Throughout the growing seasons, there will be times when plants are mostly foliage, or when their flowers have died back. So potting up some annuals is an excellent way to have colour in the garden while perennials are resting.

Pots also give you an opportunity to grow plants that wouldn't thrive in your garden soil, so if you have poor soil, you can grow your favourite plants in containers and give them the type of soil they need to flourish.

Drainage & room to grow

The main things to keep in mind when picking pots are drainage and room to grow. Especially in rainy Ireland, drainage is critical; if pots become too wet, roots can rot and disease can develop. You can upcycle all sorts of items into stunning flower displays: old sinks, furniture, buckets and bins can be used as containers once you add drainage holes.

To add drainage holes, grab your drill and a suitable drill bit. Depending on the size of the container, drill three or four evenly spaced small holes on the bottom. These holes will help water to drain freely from the pot and stop the soil from becoming waterlogged.

Before adding soil, I like to put some broken terracotta pieces over the holes to stop the soil from getting stuck and clogging the drainage holes. In winter, I also raise the container off the ground with pot feet for further drainage.

Soil

Visiting the garden centre and seeing all the soil varieties available can be overwhelming. Potting composts are different to the garden compost you make at home; they often contain a blend of ingredients like grit, loam and coir.

When adding compost to a container, I like to mix in either perlite, vermiculite or grit to help with drainage. Perlite and vermiculite both enhance the soil's structure, but they are different: vermiculite helps to retain water, while perlite increases drainage. So when planting herbs, which love well-drained Mediterranean soil and hate being soggy, I would add perlite. But if I have a thirsty astilbe in a container, I would mix some vermiculite into the soil instead.

Creating a show garden container

I watch my favourite garden programmes religiously each week, and from them I learned a helpful tip for planting up a container: pillar, filler and spiller. You want to choose a tall, upright plant (the pillar) for the centre of the container, fill in around it with mid-sized or bushy plants (the filler), and finally add trailing or cascading plants (the spiller) to spill over the edges. Following this rule creates a balanced and visually appealing arrangement in your container.

Another thing I love to do is shake wildflower seeds into a bucket in late spring and let Mother Nature create a mini container meadow that the insects will adore.

Caring for your container

Containers dry out faster than borders. I water weekly, but if it's particularly hot and sunny, I will water every second day. Check the soil to see if it is moist before you start watering, as it is easy to overwater. Small pots (especially terracotta pots) will dry out much quicker than larger containers, so prioritise watering them more often.

From spring to autumn, I suggest adding a liquid feed once a week as the soil's nutrients can deplete over time. And every year or two, I will replenish the compost in a pot, especially if it is growing a tree or shrub. To do this, remove the plant and take out as much old compost as possible before repotting and adding new potting compost. You can also mulch the top of the compost to prevent the soil from spilling over when watering.

Cut Flowers

One of my favourite treats is a bunch of fresh cut flowers for my kitchen. They give me such joy as I drink my tea in the morning, and they instantly brighten up any space. Over the years, I realised that growing flowers that are suitable for cutting in my own garden was a great cost-cutter, and it made my garden look pretty too!

Depending on the shop, a cut flower bouquet can cost anything from €10 up to €100. Instead, you can spend that money on perennial plants and grow them at home throughout the seasons. You don't need a huge space either, as you can grow them within your flower borders, in containers or in raised beds.

Tips for cutting

My favourite time to cut flowers is first thing in the morning. I make a mug of tea, fill a bucket with fresh water, and head out with my snips. I pick my faves and plop them into the water. If you are heading to work and don't have time to arrange them right away, put the bucket of fresh flowers in a cool spot, out of direct sunlight, and arrange them when you return home. Cutting flowers in the morning or evening, when plants are well hydrated, helps to prevent wilting. It's best to avoid cutting in the middle of a hot day.

Choose fresh, undamaged flowers with sturdy stems. Use clean and sharp gardening snips to avoid damaging stems and hindering water absorption. Cutting stems at a 45-degree angle helps them stay hydrated and upright in the vase. Remove lower foliage from the stems – these can rot in the water.

Clean your vase and fill it with fresh water. Some people add a splash of bleach to the water to kill bacteria – you can also add flower food or a teaspoon of sugar at this stage.

Now for the fun part: arranging your freshly cut flowers. Use a variety of flowers in different colours, textures and heights, and trim stems as needed. I love mixing foliage and grasses into my bouquets, as they add some height and fullness.

I am guilty of putting cut flowers on a sunny window sill, but they will last longer out of direct sunlight. Try to keep away from any radiators or heating vents too. To keep cut flowers fresh, change the water every two days and trim the stems at an angle. Check the water level in the mornings, remove any flowers that have started to wilt and pop them into the compost.

Plants to choose

I grow flowers that I can use from spring to early autumn. In the winter, I find that I use more foliage and fewer blossoming flowers. Below I have listed the common plant names, but there are many different varieties of each one. You can grow most of these easily from seed or bulb. Once established, you can take cuttings and divide from the parent plant to increase the size of your cut flower garden over time.

Spring

Allium	Hyacinth
Aquilegia	Tulip
Daffodil	Lilac
Honesty	

When I plant my spring bulbs, I always add a few extra to use for cut flowers. With tulips and daffodils, for example, you want to let the foliage die back and turn yellow, as the plant sends nutrients back down into the bulb to store for next year's growth. By cutting these flowers for a vase, you restrict the bulb's chances of coming back strong next year. This is why I grow some extras just for cutting, and then I admire the ones in the borders from the kitchen window.

I also love to grow spring bulbs in terracotta pots. Smaller spring plants like crocus and muscari don't really work as cut flowers, but they look amazing growing in a small pot. You can dress the soil with some sphagnum moss and create an adorable tablescape with different-sized pots and varieties of bulbs.

Summer into autumn (a starter list!)

Perennials

Achillea	Foxglove (biennial)
Astrantia	Gypsophila
Agastache	Hydrangea
Chamomile	Lavender
Campanula	Lupin
Dahlia	Rose
Delphinium	Rudbeckia (cone flowers)
Echinacea	Shasta daisy

I try to remove only one third of the flowers at a time, leaving the other flowers for the bees to enjoy. When cutting roses and hydrangeas, double-check if the particular variety grows on old wood or new, as cutting too much can hinder next year's growth. For example, mophead hydrangeas (the really common ones) grow on last year's wood, so try to cut only a portion of the shrub. Varieties like *Hydrangea paniculata* and *Hydrangea aborescens*, meanwhile, produce flowers on new wood, so you can take more stems for your bouquets without affecting next year's blooms.

Annuals

Antirrhinum (snapdragon)	*Sweet pea*
Cosmos	*Zinnia*
Sunflowers	*Native wildflower seed mixes*

Annuals are fantastic for filling gaps in your borders. Once deadheaded regularly, they will flower all summer long and are easy to grow from seed. Around St Patrick's Day, I gather my seed packets, clean the old seed trays and start sowing. By early May, they are ready to be potted or planted out – but watch out for a late frost, as most annuals are tender. Once autumn comes and growth slows down, I let them go to seed for the birds to enjoy over winter (and collect some seeds for next year).

Foliage, herbs and grasses

Sometimes I will potter around the wild bushes growing over the wall and cut a few sprigs of foliage for my arrangements. I also grow eucalyptus in a pot, which smells amazing. When it comes to trees and hedges, I have yet to learn their names and I have limited knowledge about them, but I do know their foliage is fantastic for filling gaps in my bouquets! So, don't be afraid to add some fern leaves, wild grasses or scented herbs. Experiment, have fun and don't worry about getting it perfect. Enjoy the journey of growing, cutting and then admiring the fruits of your labour.

Easy Window Mirrors

I stumbled across some old glass window frames while rummaging through a salvage yard. I adored the shape and the chippy paint, and I thought I could use them to add some interest to my garden. I'm a big fan of gardens full of trinkets and treasure! My first idea was to add a mirrored panel to the back of the windows, as I had some spare pieces in storage. However, they were slightly too small and made the window very heavy. When chatting with people on my YouTube channel, I was given the idea to use mirrored spray paint instead. (If you read my first book, you might remember the mirrored vases.) So I headed out to pick up a can of mirrored paint and give it a go.

Old windows can have many uses in the garden. You can make a greenhouse or a cold frame, or get creative and turn them into wall planters. You could even remove the glass and use them as a trellis for climbing plants or a backdrop in a seating area. But for now, let's turn these windows into mirrors!

While mirrored spray may not have the same vibrancy as a genuine mirror, it offers a nice level of reflection and creates the impression of spaciousness. Be careful not to place your mirror in an area that gets intense sunlight as it may be a fire hazard. And position it close to the ground so as not to confuse the birds!

What you need

Lead paint tester kit (optional)
Glass cleaner and microfibre cloth
Painter's tape
Mirror effect spray

- If you don't know how old the windows are, test the paint for lead before working on them, especially if it is chippy and deteriorated. Lead paint was banned in Ireland in 1980, but best to be sure.
- I wanted to keep the aged look of my windows, so I only cleaned the glass panels to prep them for the spray paint. I used a glass cleaner and microfibre cloth to thoroughly remove any dirt and smudges.
- Tape off surrounding areas before lightly misting two coats of mirrored spray paint onto one side of the glass. (I sprayed mine onto the back.) Allow each coat to dry thoroughly.
- Remove the painter's tape, and there you have it! You've turned a glass window into a mirrored one.
- I had some leftover ceramic paint from the tile project in the kitchen section, so I used a stencil to paint some flowers on the front of the glass. Flick to page 21 to find out how!

Brick Effect Floor & Wall

After saving my pennies for what felt like ages, I was so excited to finally get my dream greenhouse in my garden. Unfortunately, I had blown the budget on the structure, so I had to get creative with the floor.

I adore red brick floors and pathways – they have such a timeless feel – and I knew this look would complement my cottage-style garden perfectly. However, once I priced up tiles and materials, I realised my dream floor was out of reach, so I needed to find a way to do it on a budget.

Some YouTube viewers suggested stencilling the floor, which is a great option. I dug up an old Martha Stewart video where she made a faux brick stencil from sponges, adjusted the technique, took the plunge – and stencilled my floor in a brick effect.

What you need

Outdoor paint in white
Sponge roller and tray
Yellow decorator's sponge
Outdoor wall paint in reddish and brown
Clear floor varnish

- This project works best on a concrete surface like mine, but you could try it on wood. In that case, use an outdoor paint suitable for wood.
- I painted the whole floor with white outdoor paint before painting the bricks. A roller is perfect for this bit.
- Now for the fun part: creating fake bricks. Cut a sponge into a rectangular brick shape and use this as your stencil. Mix the reddish and brown paints together in a paint tray until you have a nice brick colour. Press the sponge into the paint and then press it onto the floor.
- Lay the 'bricks' in a pattern of your liking. If you are feeling brave, herringbone would look great.
- Once you finish the floor, apply one or two coats of clear varnish to help your paint job last longer.
- My floor is roughly three years old, and I haven't had to repaint it yet. I mop it with warm soapy water whenever it gets muddy. My floor is protected from the elements though, so if you were to try this on decking or a patio, it might need repainting sooner.

Feature wall

I also had a bare white wall in my garden that I wanted to break up, so I decided to do the brick effect there too. I followed the same steps but skipped the clear varnish. I added an outdoor mirror that resembled a window to create a whimsical feature. Adding mirrors is a great way to make a small garden look bigger, and your flowers look so pretty in the reflection. If you're worried about the mirror reflecting light and damaging plants, position it in a shady part of the border.

Vertical Gardens

When rambling around and visiting garden shows, I picked up on an ever-growing trend for vertical wall planting. 'Living walls' are a great way to create more growing space, especially if you have a small garden or even a balcony.

A vertical wall planter is a gardening container you can mount on a wall or other vertical surface. It usually has several pockets or compartments. This kind of planter is perfect for urban gardening, as it allows you to grow plants in a compact and space-saving manner. Vertical wall planters come in different styles and materials, from contemporary and polished designs to rustic and natural-looking planters made from wood or woven materials.

You can purchase vertical planter kits, which vary in price. Some expensive kits will come with built-in watering systems, which make it easier to maintain. Or you can make a budget option, like I did, from some old rain guttering I got from my neighbour's skip!

What you need

Old rain guttering
Brackets
Ends for rain gutter
Drill and drill bits
Potting compost and grit
Annuals, sedums or succulents

- I got lucky and found my rain gutters, brackets and ends in my neighbour's skip while they were renovating their house. You can also keep an eye on second-hand or freebie websites, or there might be a reuse/recycle centre near you.
- I began by giving my gutters a good clean. While it can be tempting to skip this step, it's an important one to prevent plant diseases. Old gutters, especially ones made from UPVC, scrub up perfectly with warm soapy water.
- Using my drill, I drilled holes into the base of the gutters for drainage. This is vital to prevent the roots from becoming too wet and rotting. You can get end caps for the gutters that clip on and stop the soil from falling out. I didn't get enough end caps from my neighbour's skip, in case you're wondering why not all my pipes have them!

- I positioned my planters on a concrete wall, as once I added the soil, they became heavy – the concrete wall could handle the weight.

- I drilled in my brackets and added the gutters to the wall. If you are on a solo DIY mission, like I was, fill with soil after mounting to avoid heavy lifting.

- You will be limited in the plants you can grow as these rain pipes are quite shallow. However, some plants will tolerate it, like sedums, succulents and some varieties of annuals. As it was heading for autumn when I built mine, I decided to do winter violas and frost-hardy sedums for some colour. In summer, I will add pansies and let the violas spill over the edge, giving me a mini floral wall.

- Sedums like well-drained soil and sitting in heavy, wet soil will cause their roots to rot, so I added some grit to the potting compost.

- As the gutters are shallow, they will need some extra attention during hot spells to prevent the soil from drying out. Just like hanging baskets, you will need to water more frequently, and you can feed them once a week with a liquid feed to keep the plants healthy.

- You can also use recycled rain pipes like these as seed trays – just add those drainage holes! – or even as a window box.

Bangin' Bird Box

Nothing gives me more joy than watching the wild birds darting around my garden. Over the years, I've witnessed blackbirds making their homes in overgrown ivy, starlings flying in and out of their lodgings in my neighbour's roof tiles, and young robins flying the nest.

Not only do wild birds serenade us as we potter around outside, but they are also the gardener's best friend, helping to control pests, spread seeds and even pollinate plants.

Creating a bird box is a fun way to practise your woodworking skills. Don't worry if your edges are a little wonky – I have a few wonky corners myself! Practice makes perfect, and the birds will be okay with our dodgy woodworking skills as long as the edges are smooth. As with other woodworking projects in the book, we're going to work in centimetres/millimetres here for precision.

What you need

Wood
Measuring tape
Jigsaw or hand saw
32 mm flat drill bit
Fine grit sandpaper
Woodworking clamps
Drill and exterior wood screws
Screwdriver
Hinges
Hook and eye latch
Outdoor wood stain (optional)

- Cedar, pine or cypress are great choices for this one, and your wood should be at least 15 mm thick.
- You can adjust the diameter of the hole to attract different birds. For example, a diameter of 25 mm will attract coal tits and blue tits; 28 mm would be good for great tits and tree sparrows; and 32 mm welcomes house sparrows. For my bird box, I went with a 32 mm hole as I had noticed many house sparrows visiting my garden and I would love to see them set up a home.
- Pop on your safety goggles, then start cutting your wood using a hand saw or an electric jigsaw.

  ◊ Cut one front piece 12 x 19 cm
  ◊ Cut one back piece 12 x 19 cm

◊ Cut two side pieces, 7 x 19 cm

◊ Cut one bottom piece, 12 x 12 cm

◊ Cut one top piece, 14 x 14 cm

- Before assembling the box, use the flat drill bit to cut your entrance hole on the front piece of wood.
- Smooth any rough edges with a fine-grit sandpaper. Pay particular attention to the wood around the entrance hole, which shouldn't have any sharp edges or splinters.
- Use woodworking clamps to hold the wood in place as you drill the pieces together. I began by attaching the front piece to the bottom base, then the back part and sides. Before drilling in the screws, I drilled a pilot hole, as this helps prevent the wood from splitting.
- To make it easier to clean the nesting box, use two small hinges on the top piece. Attach the hinges to the back and top pieces with small screws.
- Attach a hook and eye latch to the top and side pieces. A hook and eye latch will help stop predators from opening the nesting box.
- I painted the outside of my box with a water-based wood stain to help protect it from the elements. However, I left the inside unpainted as I wanted to use as few chemicals as possible.
- To fix the box to the post, I drilled it through the back and into the fence post so it would be secure from the wind. You can also use wire or a strong metal hook to attach it to a fence or wall.

Locating your nesting box

Position your bird box in a quiet, sheltered area that is out of the direct sunshine and protected from harsh wind. Make sure it's away from any feeding tables, as birds attracted to the food table may be off-putting for the nesting birds. Ideally, locate your bird box at least 2 metres from the ground to ensure predators like cats can't disturb or even look into the nest box.

Many birds will start the search for a nesting site from February onwards, so it's best to pop up your birdhouse before the breeding season begins.

Caring for your new bird box

It can be exciting when our feathered friends choose our bird boxes to reside in. However, you should never peep inside the box as you risk the parents abandoning the nest. It is a good idea to clean out any old nesting material or eggs to prevent parasites from affecting next year's brood. You can open the bird box from the end of October to clean it.

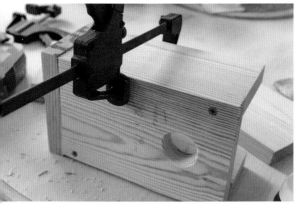

Cosy Lounge Cushion

It can be tricky to find the right size cushion for an outdoor chair, so let me share how I created this cute foldable one. You can use it on a lounge chair, as a mat on the grass, or even as a seat of its own. It has a carrying handle, making it the perfect picnic cushion.

For this project, I recycled an old blanket I had stashed in the hot press. (Anyone else unable to resist a pretty patterned blanket even though they have way too many?) I loved the patchwork design but I rarely used it, so I decided to give it a new purpose in the garden. Don't worry if you don't have a spare blanket in your stash, as any cotton or polycotton material will do. You could use a waterproof fabric, but I find those less comfy to sit on.

I will leave measurements below for the size I created, but feel free to tweak this design to suit your own needs.

What you need

An old blanket or material of your choice
Measuring tape
Fabric marker and ruler
Fabric scissors
Sewing pins
Thread
Sewing machine
Two pillows or filler
Hand sewing needle

- Begin by measuring the length and width of the chair that you would like your cushion to sit on. I cut two pieces of fabric to 17½ x 57½ in (44½ x 146 cm), including a seam allowance of ½ in (1¼ cm).
- If using recycled material, make sure to wash and iron the material before sewing. Transfer the measurements onto your fabric using your fabric marker and ruler and cut.
- I added a strap on either end of the cushion, making it easy to fold up and carry. This is optional so if you'd rather go without, skip the next few steps! Mine is a chunky strap that measures 3½ x 15½ in (9 x 40 cm). You could always use a thick ribbon or cord instead.
- To create a strap, cut four strips of material. These will make two straps, one for each end of the cushion.

- Place one piece of fabric on top of the other with the patterned (right) sides facing each other. Do a straight line of stitching down both of the long edges, leaving ends open.
- Turn the material the right way out.
- Also, I did a topstitch down the two long edges, but this is purely decorative and is optional.
- Now to put all of the pieces together. Lay one of the cushion pieces on a flat surface with the patterned (right) side facing upwards.
- Position the straps on either end of the cushion piece, facing inwards, and pin them securely. Make sure they are spaced evenly on both ends (see photo).
- Next, lay the other cushion piece on top, with the right (patterned) side facing down. The two right sides are now facing each other, with the straps sandwiched in between. Use lots of pins to secure the fabric in place.
- Now, the most important part! Leave an opening on one of the long sides for you to turn the cushion the right way out, making sure it's also large enough to insert your cushions or filler. But don't panic – you can always use a seam ripper to make it bigger.
- Machine stitch all around the cushion, except for this gap.
- Carefully insert your pillows or filler. If you have a lot of fabric scraps in your stash, you can tear these into small pieces and use them as filler.

- Fold the hem of the opening inward; this will ensure that it aligns with the seam allowance on both sides of the stitch.
- Grab your needle and thread and close the gap with a ladder stitch (see page 200).
- Secure by making a final stitch and passing the needle through the loop to create a knot. Trim any excess thread, and you're done!

If you see any grey clouds, bring your cushion inside.
I find storing fabric items like this in a shed over winter
can cause mould, so indoors is best.

Tiled Garden Table

I am always curious to work with new materials, but tiling is one skill that used to intimidate me! There was a trend for tiled tables online a while back, so I took the idea, tweaked it and dived in.

This is a fun way to use up leftover tiles and a great beginner tiling project that will help you grow in confidence. Also, it's a nice alternative to painting as a way to revamp an old item.

For this project, I had an old outdoor bistro table set, and I used the tabletop as my base. I will share how I built mine, but feel free to make it your own. We'll use centimetres and millimetres here, as they're more precise.

What you need

Tiles
Sheet of MDF
Measuring tape and pencil
Clamp
Saw
Safety glasses and gloves
Manual tile cutter
Tile adhesive and grout
A notched tile adhesive spreader
Tile spacers
Decorative wood trim or tile trim
Grout float
Screws and drill

- When pulling your supplies, try to shop from the sheds and toolboxes of friends and family members first! Also, see if you can borrow tools to help keep costs down.
- I chose a smaller mosaic tile for my tabletop and these came on a mesh sheet, making it easier to cut them to size. Tiling tip! When picking tiles, you'll notice that they often have batch numbers. Try to buy tiles from the same batch, as batches can vary in colour and finish.
- To begin, measure and cut your MDF board to size. This will be the base you'll tile on. I used a 3.2 mm thick board. My tabletop measured 55 x 54 cm so I went slightly wider on the MDF, 60 x 60 cm, to make it more symmetrical and hide the wood from the old table underneath.

- Clamp your wood to a table or solid surface and cut the MDF to size using a saw. Some hardware stores offer a wood-cutting service if you are not confident cutting the wood yourself.

- To figure out how many tiles you'll need, place them on the board and play around with their positioning. Leave space for the grout in between. Once you are happy with the layout, mark any tiles that need cutting.

- There are many ways to cut tiles – I find a manual tile cutter a good option. To cut a tile on a manual cutter, start by aligning it in the tile cutter's guide and securing it in place. Apply firm pressure to the tile scorer and run it along the marked line. Next, place the scored tile on the breaker bed and apply pressure to the top handle until it snaps along the scored line. (Pop on a pair of safety gloves and glasses when cutting tiles, especially smaller mosaics, as I find they can sometimes shoot off!)

- Now you'll stick the tiles to the board. Begin by spreading your tile adhesive smoothly over the board; you can do this in smaller sections if your table is on the larger side. Then, use your notched tile adhesive spreader to even it out.

- Place the tiles onto the adhesive and lightly press. The goal is to have the tiles evenly levelled. Use tile spacers in between to keep an even grout line.

- For my edging, I cut leftover wood trim and tacked a piece to each side of the wood base. You can also use tile trim to finish off the edges of your table.

- With all the tiles and edging in place, allow the adhesive to dry. Depending on the brand you're using, this can take up to twenty-four hours.

- When the adhesive is dry, remove the tile spacers and apply the grout to the gaps between the tiles. I love using grout! It's very satisfying, like icing a cake.

- Use a grout float to smooth the grout into the gaps and wipe away excess with a damp sponge. Once you are happy with the grout, allow it to dry completely. Depending on the type of grout you're using, you may need to add a coat of sealer around three days later for extra protection.

- With the tiled tabletop now complete, secure it to the base of the table. Use screws of the proper depth so they don't penetrate the tile and crack it.

- I gave my wood trim a lick of paint to match and one last polish of the tile.

- Then it was time to pop a big mug of tea on top, admire my new table, and feel the satisfaction of trying something new.

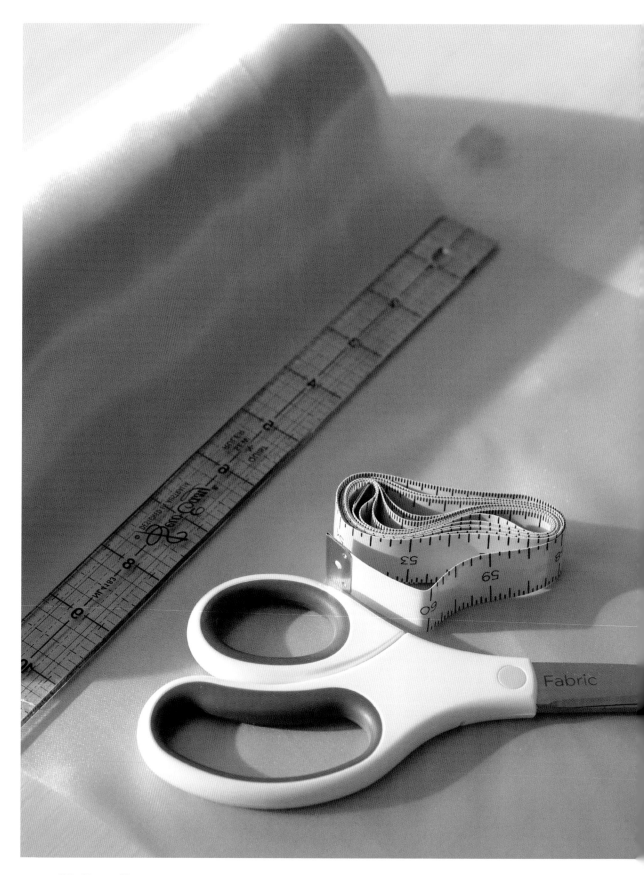

Sewing Terminology

- **Basting:** Also known as tacking. A basting stitch is a temporary long stitch that you can remove. Commonly used in dressmaking or sewing projects where you need to put in a temporary stitch before you do your final stitch.

- **Backstitch:** A reverse stitch used at the beginning and end of a seam to secure the stitches and prevent them from unravelling.

- **Bias:** Bias cut means cutting the fabric at a 45-degree angle to the straight grain. To put it simply, the material is cut at a diagonal angle. Fabric cut on the bias has more stretch and give to it. Every piece of woven fabric has two biases perpendicular to each other. Non-woven fabrics such as felt or interfacing do not have a bias.

- **Bias binding:** Also known as binding tape. Bias binding can be handmade, or you can purchase it in strips from the shop. Bias binding can be used for piping, finishing necklines and armholes, bunting and more. It is a narrow strip of fabric that has been cut on the bias, and it has more stretch, making it great for finishing curved items like necklines.

- **Binding:** To finish an edge, seam or hem of a garment.

- **Casing:** A casing is a tunnel you create to allow elastic/cord to be pulled through. For example, you would create a casing for a drawstring bag or an elastic waist skirt.

- **Dart:** A dart is used to shape a garment. You would sew a dart when dressmaking; it is commonly used around the bust and waist area.

- **Face:** The front-facing side, also known as the 'right side', is the patterned side of your fabric. Most fabrics have a distinct front and back. The front or right side is the side you want to be facing out when you complete your project.

- **Facing:** Fabric used to finish off the raw edge of a garment. It's similar to bias tape, but shaped facings are cut to match the edge they will face, while bias facings are fabric strips cut on the bias and shaped to fit the edge.

- **Fusible interfacing:** This is an interfacing fabric with glue on one or both sides, which provides structure when it is ironed onto the fabric. For example, you would use interfacing when sewing a handbag to stiffen the fabric to hold its shape.

- **Grain:** The vertical grainline runs parallel to the selvedge. The crosswise grain is at a 90-degree angle from your lengthwise grain that runs along your selvedge. The true bias grain is 45 degrees from your selvedge. Fabric cut on the true bias grain will have more stretch in it. When using a sewing pattern, you may be instructed to line up the arrow to the grain line. This is the horizontal line that is parallel to the selvedge.

- **Hem:** The folded edge of a piece of clothing. In other words, it is when you turn under and sew the edge of a piece of clothing. Your trousers, sleeve or dress would have a hem on the bottom.

- **Ladder stitch:** A stitch that can be used to invisibly close seams from the outside of the garment or item. After threading the needle, hold the fabric pieces together. Insert the needle from the backside of the fabric, bringing it up through the bottom piece only. Then, insert the needle back into the bottom fabric, bringing it up through both layers to create a small horizontal stitch. Repeat this process, making parallel stitches at equal distances, to create a ladder effect.

- **Notions:** Any small tools you need for your project. On the back of a sewing pattern, there will be details on how much fabric to purchase as well as notions. These could be buttons, zips, thread etc.

- **Pattern:** A template that you can copy from. You can get many different patterns, from dressmaking patterns to patterns for household items. Most patterns are printed on tissue paper and come in a packet with instructions for you to follow. You can also create your own patterns.

- **Piping:** A decorative trim or cord that is inserted into a seam or edge of a cushion or garment.

- **Pressing:** Using an iron to shape, flatten, and set seams and fabric.

- **Raw edge:** The unfinished fabric edge; prone to fraying, needs to be finished with a seam or hem.

- **Right side:** The right side of a piece of fabric is the printed or front side. You may be instructed to sew your right sides facing together, which means you sew the two patterned pieces together.

- **Seam:** A seam is a line where a thread holds two pieces of fabric together. So your hem is the fabric that is folded under, and the stitching is your seam.

- **Seam allowance:** Your seam allowance is the area between the edge of your fabric and your line of stitching. If you sew too close to the edge, your seam may weaken and unravel. In most commercial patterns, your seam allowance can range from ¼ in (⅔ cm) to ⅝ inch (1½ cm). You can use the throat plate on your sewing machine or a magnetic seam guide to help you with your seam allowance.

- **Seam ripper:** A tool used to remove stitches, often used to undo mistakes or alter sewing projects.

- **Selvedge/Selvage:** The tightly woven edge of your fabric. When you buy fabric, you may notice the selvedge, as it can have numbers on it. It is hard to fray and runs parallel to the vertical grain line.

- **Stitch:** A loop or series of loops made with a needle and thread to join fabric together.

- **Topstitch:** A topstitch is a line of stitching designed to be seen on the right side of your fabric. Most common on necklines and hems.

- **Wrong side:** The wrong side of your fabric is the opposite side of the patterned or right side of your fabric. It is the back of your piece of fabric.

Furniture Painting Guide

Revamping old furniture with a fresh coat of paint is a fun way to unleash your creativity and personalise your decor. With so many paint options and techniques out there, it can feel overwhelming, but don't worry! I have put together this guide to break it all down and help you get a pro paint job first go. Make sure to bookmark these pages for easy reference as you dive into your furniture makeover projects. Happy painting!

Types of paint

Primer: Ensuring that your paint job is durable, long-lasting, and has a professional finish starts with the right primer. A primer provides a solid foundation for the topcoat to adhere to, preventing issues such as peeling, chipping and lifting. Different primers are available for different surfaces, for example wood, tile or metal. When painting flat pack furniture, the surface can be a veneered MDF, so use a primer designed to adhere to MDF/difficult surfaces.

Undercoat: If you're painting over an old layer of paint, an undercoat can be a useful alternative to a primer, especially when transitioning from a dark to a light colour. Using an undercoat means you'll need fewer coats of topcoat, and it can also act as a minor filler, creating a smooth base. Both primers and undercoats typically have a matte, chalky finish.

Topcoat: The topcoat is the final layer of paint. It comes in different finishes, which I'll explain below. Generally, I apply one primer layer followed by two topcoat layers in my chosen colour.

Paint finishes

Chalk: Chalk paint offers excellent adhesion and is perfect for achieving an aged French effect. Some brands even market their chalk paint as a 'no-prep' paint, allowing you to apply it directly to wood without priming. However, the piece will still need sealing with wax or varnish, and you will need to prime knotty or dark-stained wood to avoid oils bleeding through.

Eggshell: Eggshell provides a low-sheen look. It's self-sealing, so there's no need to apply varnish on top. It's also tough and wipeable, making it ideal for kitchen cabinets and high-traffic areas.

Gloss: Gloss offers a high-sheen finish and is durable and hardwearing. It's often used for doors and skirting boards as it's easy to clean. Like satin and eggshell, it's self-sealing and won't require varnish.

Satin: Satin finish falls between eggshell and gloss, offering a lower sheen than gloss. Once you've applied two coats, there's no need to apply varnish over it. Satin is also durable and easy to clean, making it a popular choice.

My personal preference is for either satin or eggshell. While I appreciate the look of chalk paint, I find that it doesn't wear well over time, and gloss is too shiny for my liking. Satin provides a nice sprayed feel, and with proper prep, it wears well. Of course, there's no right or wrong choice, and it's always good to have an open mind when selecting paint. Paint brands typically have plenty of information on their websites, but if you're struggling to decide, don't hesitate to ask a stockist for advice. Your local decorating shop has a wealth of knowledge and info, so don't be afraid to ask.

Water- vs oil-based

Oil-based paints use oil as a base, dry more slowly, have a strong odour, and require solvents for clean-up. They are durable but may turn yellow over time.

Water-based paints use water as a base, dry faster, have lower levels of odour and VOCs, and are easy to clean with water and soap. They may be less durable but they have better colour retention.

Consider factors such as drying time, odour, environmental impact, durability and ease of use when choosing between oil-based and water-based paints for your project. I personally use water-based paints as much as possible.

What are VOCs?

When shopping for paint, you might notice a VOC symbol on the back or side of your can. Volatile Organic Compounds are chemicals that can be released from products like paints and enter the air, potentially contributing to indoor air pollution. VOCs emitted during paint drying and curing can cause health issues like respiratory irritation, headache and allergies when inhaled.

Low-VOC or zero-VOC paints have been developed to address concerns about VOCs contributing to outdoor air pollution and environmental damage, making them eco-friendly and promoting safer indoor air quality.

Painting furniture

To get the most out of your upcycled furniture, it's important to follow proper prep, prime, paint and curing steps. Taking the time to do it right will result in a professional finish that will stand the test of time. I know how tempting it is to skip the prep and prime stages and go straight to the painting, but while it may not be the most thrilling part of the process, proper prep is crucial for a durable and chip-free paint job.

Clean: Get your furniture ready for painting by giving it a thorough cleaning with a degreaser or warm, soapy water. You'll be amazed at the grime and oil that can come off with a simple rinse. A sponge or wire sponge works great, especially for tougher stains.

Sand: After cleaning, it's time to lightly sand the furniture surface using medium-grit sandpaper. Whether you do it by hand or with an electrical sander, the goal is to create a smooth base for the primer and paint to adhere to. No need to sand it bare, just give it a gentle scratch. Don't forget to wipe away the dust with a lint-free cloth before moving on to painting.

Fill: Depending on your project, something I like to do these days is to use decorators caulk or wood filler. When painting skirting boards and door frames, I find filling in gaps with some decorators caulk gives a professional and seamless finish.

Prime: Using a primer is highly recommended for bare wood or never-before-painted furniture. It creates a perfect base for your topcoat and prevents stains and oils from seeping through. A shellac-based primer is ideal for dark wood or knotty pine. If your furniture has been previously painted, make sure to sand away any old, flaky paint and use an undercoat instead of a primer. A specialised primer can help with paint adhesion for challenging surfaces like tile or MDF. I typically apply one coat of primer using a small roller, but if stains are still visible, a second coat may be needed. Always refer to the application guidelines on the back of the can for the best results.

Paint: Now comes the exciting part – applying your topcoat! You can use a roller or brush for this step. Two coats are sufficient for most projects, but additional coats may be necessary if you observe uneven coverage or patchiness. If needed, you can lightly sand away any paint drips or uneven areas between coats. Allow each coat to dry completely before applying the next one to ensure a smooth finish. Patience pays off in the end!

Cure: Speaking of patience, don't rush the curing process! Many paint chips occur because the paint hasn't fully cured. Although it may feel touch-dry after a few hours, paint needs several days or weeks to completely cure and become durable. Just like when you paint your nails and they smudge despite feeling dry, the same applies to paint. Allow a week or more before using your furniture, especially if it's in a high-traffic area of your home. For example, protect a table with a tablecloth for a few days before using.

Don't forget, many topcoats are self-sealing, so you won't need varnish or wax. However, if you're working with chalk paint, which can be challenging to clean and prone to discolouration, you'll want to seal it with a clear varnish or wax for added protection. Keep this in mind to ensure a beautiful and durable finish for your upcycled furniture!

Removing old paint

There are lots of reasons why you might want to remove paint from a piece of furniture. Perhaps you've come across a great second-hand piece, but you're not a fan of the colour. Or maybe you've made a mistake in your project and want to start fresh. Here are some options for removing paint.

Heat gun: These look like hairdryers but are more powerful. They work best on latex paint but may not be as effective with chalk paint. Start by applying heat in small areas and use a scraper to gently lift off the bubbling paint. Continue this process until you reach the wood underneath. After removing the old paint, use a degreaser to deep clean the piece and check for any damage or areas that need repair. Smooth and even out the wood using a sander or sanding block.

Paint stripper: In recent years, there are more environmentally friendly, water-based chemical strippers available in the market. While cheaper chemical paint strippers can be challenging to use and have a strong odour, eco-friendly paint strippers are easier to use and work well with tricky chalk paint. Apply a layer of paint stripper to the furniture using a brush and allow it to work its magic, causing the paint to crack and bubble. Use a scraper to remove the old paint, and then clean off the sticky residue with a bucket of soapy water and a wire sponge.

When stripping furniture, always wear a mask and gloves to protect your skin and lungs. Vintage furniture may have old paint that contains lead, so it's important to use a lead test kit from a hardware store or online if you're unsure. Lead-based paint was banned in Ireland in 1980 and in the UK in 1992, but it's better to be cautious and check first.

After stripping, you have various options for tone and finish. If you like the wood underneath, you can apply oil, wax or varnish to protect it. Alternatively, you can use a wood stain to change the tone, which is popular in mid-century and boho decor trends that feature warm tones, textures and patterns.

Painting techniques

Using a brush: This is the most common painting technique for furniture. It involves using a brush to apply paint in even strokes, typically in the direction of the wood grain. Brush painting allows for precise control over the application of paint and can result in a smooth, even finish. If you follow me online, you will know that I am a fan of using old make-up and art brushes on projects, as they give a smooth finish.

Spray: Spray painting furniture involves using a spray gun or aerosol spray paint to evenly coat the surface. It can result in a smooth, professional-looking finish and is especially useful for covering large areas quickly. However, it requires careful preparation, such as proper ventilation and masking, to avoid overspray and achieve a smooth result. Using a paint roller can give a similar effect.

Distressing: This technique is used to create a worn, aged look on furniture. It involves applying a base coat of paint, followed by a topcoat of a contrasting colour. Once the topcoat is partially dry, it can be sanded or scraped to reveal the base coat, creating a distressed or weathered effect.

Dry brushing: This is a painting technique where a dry brush with very little paint is lightly brushed over the surface of the furniture. This creates a textured, worn or rustic look, with some of the original wood or previous layers of paint showing through.

Stencilling: This is where you use a stencil to apply paint in a specific design or pattern.

Whitewashing: For this technique, diluted white paint is applied to the furniture, allowing some of the wood grain or previous layers of paint to show through. It creates a light, washed-out look that can give the furniture a fresh, beachy or farmhouse-inspired look.

Index

playhouses, 145–7

plumbing, 91

polycotton fabric, 25, 72, 118, 122, 191

potted plants, 70, 169–70, 175

pretty tiled tray, 35–7

primers, 19, 65, 80, 82, 86, 121, 140, 144, 145, 201, 203–4

pruning, 76

raised beds, 165, 173

rechargeable light bulbs, 70, 115

recycling, 102, 148–50, 151–3; *see also* salvaged items; upcycling

reed diffusers, 40–1

rugs, 70, 151

salvaged items, 139–41, 165, 183; *see also* recycling; upcycling

sanding, 16, 47–9, 56, 82, 86, 104, 140, 144, 188, 203

satin fabric, 96

satin finish paint, 80, 140, 202

satinwood paint, 144

scratching post, 148–50

scrunchies, 93–5

seating areas, 130, 163, 165

second-hand items, 16, 20, 33, 102–4, 128, 142, 145, 165, 183

seeds, 166, 174, 176

sewing terminology, 199–200

shelves, 16, 32–4, 92, 130, 147

shoe storage, 69, 130

shrubs, 163, 166, 170

silk fabric, 96

sinks, 19–20

smart lightbulbs, 70, 131

soil, 76, 160–3, 169–70, 185

spray paint, 142, 179, 205

stair runners, 84–7

stencils, 21–2, 140, 179, 181, 205

Stewart, Martha, 181

storage
  bathroom, 92
  children's room storage, 128, 130
  hallway, 69
  hidden storage, 69
  kitchen, 33–4
  shoe storage, 69, 130
  storage benches, 69, 130

sugar soap, 82, 84, 139, 140

tables
  children's table and chairs, 139–41
  console tables, 69
  dining tables, 20
  kitchen tables, 20
  tiled garden table, 194–7

tack strips, 83, 87

taps, 19–20, 91, 92

tile spacers, 37, 196

tiled garden table, 194–7

tiles
  bathroom, 92
  cutting, 196
  front steps, 82
  grouting, 37, 92, 196
  kitchen backsplashes, 19
  mosaic tiles, 195
  painting, 19, 21–2, 92
  peel-and-stick tiles, 19
  pretty tiled tray, 35–7
  tiled garden table, 194–7

towel scrunchies, 93–5

towels, 92, 93, 99

trays, 35–7

trees, 166, 169, 170, 176

underlay, 83, 87

upcycled bottle lamp, 113–15

upcycling, 33, 113–15, 128, 139–41; *see also* recycling; salvaged items

varnish, 46, 49, 105, 115, 140, 181, 204

vegetables, 165, 166, 169

velcro, 99, 101, 147, 153

vermiculite, 170

vertical gardens, 183–5

vinegar, 27–9

vinyl stickers, 19

wainscoting, 60–5

wall decals, 130

wall plugs, 33, 34

wallpaper steamers, 55

wallpaper stripping, 54–5

wallpapering, 51–4

water butts, 165

watering, 165, 170

wax
  candle wax, 59
  wood-sealing wax, 46, 49, 104–5, 204

whitewashing, 20, 104, 144, 205

wild flowers, 163, 170

window mirrors, 178–9, 182

wine bottle candles, 56–9

wood panelling, 60–5, 119–21

wood staining, 16, 37, 46, 47–9, 84, 104

wreaths, 76–9

YouTube, 166, 179, 181